THE BRONTËS

A BEGINNER'S GUIDE

STEVE EDDY

Series Editors
Rob Abbott & Charlie Bell

Hodder & Stoughton

A MEMBER OF THE HODDER HEADLINE GROUP

Acknowledgements

My thanks to Professor Shigeyuki Oenokei for information on the Brontës popularity in Japan, and to Maki Miyashita for tracking him down.

Orders: please contact Bookpoint Ltd, 130 Milton Park, Abingdon, Oxon OX14 4SB.
Telephone: (44) 01235 827720, Fax: (44) 01235 400454. Lines are open from 9.00–6.00,
Monday to Saturday, with a 24-hour message answering service.
You can also order through our website www.madaboutbooks.co.uk

British Library Cataloguing in Publication Data
A catalogue record for this title is available from The British Library

ISBN 0 340 85729 3

First published 2003
Impression number   10 9 8 7 6 5 4 3 2 1
Year 2007 2006 2005 2004 2003

Cover photo by courtesy of the National Portrait Gallery, London.
Typeset by Transet Limited, Coventry, England.
Printed in Great Britain for Hodder & Stoughton Educational, a division of Hodder Headline
Plc, 338 Euston Road, London NW1 3BH by Cox & Wyman, Reading, Berks.

CONTENTS

How to use this book

The *Beginner's Guide* series aims to introduce readers to major writers of the past 500 years. It is assumed that readers will begin with little or no knowledge and will want to go on to explore the subject in other ways.

BEGIN READING THE AUTHORS

This book is a companion guide to major works of the Brontës, it is not a substitute for reading the books themselves. It would be useful if you read some of the works in parallel, so that you can put theory into practice. This *Beginner's Guide* is divided into sections. After considering how to approach the authors' work and a brief biography, we go on to explore some of the main writings and themes before examining some critical approaches. The survey finishes with suggestions for further reading and possible areas of further study.

HOW TO APPROACH UNFAMILIAR OR DIFFICULT TEXTS

Coming across a new writer may seem daunting, but do not be put off. The trick is to persevere. Much good writing is multi-layered and complex. It is precisely this diversity and complexity which makes literature rewarding and exhilarating.

Literary work often needs to be read more than once and in different ways. These ways can include: a leisurely and superficial reading to get the main ideas and narrative; a slower more detailed reading focusing on the nuances of the text and on what appear to be key passages; and reading in a random way, moving back and forth through the text to examine different aspects, such as themes, narrative or characterization.

VOCABULARY AND CHAPTER REFERENCES

You will see that keywords and unfamiliar terms are set in **bold** text. These words are also defined and explained in the glossary to be found at the back of the book.

This book is a tool to help you appreciate a key figure in literature. We hope you enjoy reading it and find it useful.

✳ ✳ ✳ *SUMMARY* ✳ ✳ ✳

To maximize the use of this book:

- Read the authors' work.

- Read it several times in different ways.

- Be open to innovative or unusual forms of writing.

- Persevere.

Rob Abbott and Charlie Bell

Why Read the Brontës Today?

PASSION AND COMMITMENT

The outstanding quality of the Brontë novels and poems is their passionate intensity. The passion burns brightest in the doomed love of Cathy and Heathcliff in *Wuthering Heights*. At its lowest level we see it in Heathcliff's violence towards Isabella, the bride he takes in place of Catherine in a twisted act of revenge, or in Catherine 'dashing her head against the arm of the sofa, and grinding her teeth so that you might fancy she would crash them into splinters'. But elsewhere the passion is tempered with idealism, as in Catherine's assertion to Nelly the housekeeper: 'I *am* Heathcliff.'

Heathcliff himself is committed to Catherine even beyond the grave. This passion of tragic love, while compelling in itself, might be seen as negative, but fortunately we see new hope dawning with the younger Catherine and her wooing of the not-quite-ruined Hareton Earnshaw. There is also a strong element of spiritual yearning in this passion, one which finds a purer form in Emily's poems.

Charlotte's passion is less raw. The heroine of *Jane Eyre* has a slow fuse. As a victimized child she finally explodes in rebellion against her aunt's injustice and neglect. As an adult she slowly comes to love the testy and imperious Rochester, and her passion finally bursts out in the wonderful orchard scene, appropriately followed by a violent storm. Yet hers is a passion tempered by realistic expectations: she is in fact a very modern lover.

Anne Brontë's passion is of a different order. We see it in her commitment to social ideals, such as the plight of Helen Huntingdon, abused by an alcoholic husband, or in the fine scene in *Agnes Grey* in which the governess heroine makes a brave stand against wanton cruelty, crushing a nest of young birds rather than let her young charge torture them to death.

GENRE AND CHARACTERIZATION

Jane Eyre and *Wuthering Heights* are both, at one level, **Gothic** Romantic novels. The Gothic **Romance**, with its elements of mystery, the supernatural, dreams, death and doom, has an enduring appeal that appears, for example in the novels of Daphne de Maurier (*Rebecca* was in part based on *Jane Eyre*), Angela Carter and, more recently, Poppy Z. Brite. Closely related is the **Byronic hero**, as represented by Heathcliff and Rochester. However, the sisters take the basic genre, and the character type, and make them their own. There is little in either novel that is merely stereotypical. Even *Jane Eyre*'s Bertha Mason (the 'madwoman in the attic'), though hardly a fully rounded character, has a hideous vitality of her own.

Anne, too, provides us with a convincingly dissolute male character in Huntingdon (based on Branwell), as well as a more ideal one in the narrator Markham.

The sisters, however, are outstanding in their portrayal of strong female characters struggling to become independent in a male-dominated society. Even though in Western society there is no longer a need for an Anne Brontë to proselytize for a woman's right to a career or to divorce an abusive husband, the issues of male domination are still alive today, albeit in subtler forms.

The Brontës champion self-discovery and remaining true to oneself – again, as important now as in their time. This is frequently in relation to attempted domination by others, not just in the obvious sense, as in Heathcliff's domination of Isabella, but in the apparently benign form too, as when a besotted Rochester showers Jane with clothes and

---

KEYWORDS

Gothic: descriptive of a novel or poem focusing on the stranglehold of the past on the present, and containing suggestions of the supernatural. In the English Gothic tradition, these turn out to have rational explanations.

Romance: a novel or poem which is fantastical and focuses on high emotions rather than everyday reality.

Byronic hero: typically a proud, brooding man, of superior intellect and sensitivity, often tormented by some dark sexual crime in his past, yet rebelliously refusing to repent; based, in part, on Milton's Lucifer.

jewellery of his choice, and she responds by refusing to become his exotic slave-girl. In this they anticipate several later novelists, such as George Eliot, Thomas Hardy and D.H. Lawrence.

STRUCTURE, SYMBOLISM AND STYLE

The passion, commitment and psychological depth of the Brontë novels might still founder were it not for the sisters' inspired craftsmanship. Their careful and balanced structuring, combined with the subtle foreshadowing and echoing of events, helps to make them satisfying reading. *Wuthering Heights* is particularly well conceived structurally, its narrative viewpoint shifting between its various narrators and subtly altering in style accordingly. *Jane Eyre* is structurally less complex but equally effective. *Agnes Grey*, though less mature than these, has been praised for its perfect form.

Symbolism, too, is a vital feature. For Emily, doors and windows represent the freedom demanded (and denied) by Heathcliff and Catherine. In Charlotte's *Jane Eyre*, Rochester's house, with its madwoman in the attic, is a potent symbol for his **psyche** and moral situation, while the chestnut tree split by lightning shows the split between his pretence and the reality, as does the rending of Jane's wedding veil by the roaming Bertha.

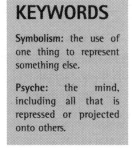

KEYWORDS

Symbolism: the use of one thing to represent something else.

Psyche: the mind, including all that is repressed or projected onto others.

The sisters are a joy to read not least because of their style. Charlotte has a special gift for imagery, as when Jane's hopes are dashed: 'ice glazed the ripe apples, drifts crushed the blowing roses; on hayfield and cornfield lay a frozen shroud' (*Jane Eyre*, Ch. 26). Emily's use of imagery is more sparing, as befits the gauntness of her setting, and often involves opposites, especially ice and fire – the latter linking Heathcliff to hellfire. Her poems are similarly intense yet restrained. Anne's style is fresh, flowing and lucid, though relatively understated. Its tone often contains a pleasing hint of irony.

All the sisters at their best show a vitality of style that reflects their commitment to life, freedom and spiritual aspiration in the face of oppression, setbacks and mortality.

UNIVERSAL APPEAL

The universal appeal of the Brontës is shown by their popularity in Japan, in many ways so different culturally from nineteenth-century England. The Japanese appreciate the passionate and unconventional love story told in *Wuthering Heights*, the enigma of Heathcliff himself, and the novel's moorland setting. The appeal of *Jane Eyre* lies in Jane's insistence on female equality, her resistance to bullying, and the atmosphere of Gothic mystery. There have been 37 Japanese editions of *Wuthering Heights* since 1922, stage adaptations have been performed in Tokyo, and a film of the novel was made by Yoshishige Yamada in 1988.

✳ ✳ ✳ SUMMARY ✳ ✳ ✳

Read the Brontës for:

- Life-affirming passionate intensity, purest in Emily, tempered by moral concerns in Charlotte, and charged with a desire for social change in Anne.

- The way they address timeless themes, such as oppression, cruelty and injustice, gender issues and spiritual striving.

- Their imaginative development of Gothic Romance and the Byronic hero, and their influence on later authors.

- Profound characterization, and especially their feisty 'modern' heroines.

- Entertaining and well-formed plots, rich symbolism and imagery, and subtle prose rhythms.

- Their universal appeal.

2 How to Approach the Brontës' Work

The Brontë sisters grew up with shared imaginative influences. It follows that they often overlap in themes and narrative techniques, while clearly showing their individuality. Before examining a passage from each sister, it is worth considering what overall similarities and differences to look for.

UNDERSTANDING THE CHARACTERS

All three sisters portray character with depth and complexity. Anne's deliberate moral purpose has led critics to undervalue her, but her main characters are complex and alive. She is also adept at introducing characters with a telling description of physical appearance and personality traits, often tinged with dry irony. One special pointer with her is how characters treat animals. You should immediately suspect anyone who kicks dogs or cats or sees young birds as fair sport for boys!

Emily's characters show sufficient psychological realism to make them believable, yet their real depth is in the mythic power of their tempestuous relationships. Charlotte's novels, especially *Jane Eyre* and *Villette*, are psychologically astute, yet they also incorporate elements of **allegory**, **myth** and **fairytale**.

WHAT'S IN A NAME?

Names often provide keys to character. In *Wuthering Heights* the nature names Heathcliff, Hareton and Hindley are set against the refined and civilized Edgar, Isabella and Linton. The first of these is also connected to Edgar in *King Lear*, the rightful heir wronged by an illegitimate brother. In *Jane Eyre* we have Rochester,

KEYWORDS

Allegory: a story whose meaning is deliberately represented in a symbol.

Myth: an ancient story involving deities which personify aspects of the universe, the human mind and the human situation.

Fairytale: a story involving magical beings and events.

whose name is that of a dissolute earl, while 'Jane' suggests 'Plain' and 'Eyre' hints at suppressed anger (ire) and a love of liberty (air). The name Lucy Snowe in *Villette* suggests its narrator's chilly emotional repression and alludes to Wordsworth's 'Lucy' poems.

NARRATIVE VIEWPOINT

To stay on top of the action in Brontë novels, it helps to remember who is speaking at any one time. This is especially the case in *Wuthering Heights*, in which Lockwood's narrative frames the main narrative delivered to him by the housekeeper, Nelly Dean. A third level also appears whenever Nelly relates what she has been told by other characters. Lockwood is identified early on as an unreliable narrator, in his darkly comic first visit to the Heights. He mistakes a pile of dead rabbits for a litter of kittens, refers to the surly young Cathy as a 'beneficent fairy' and assumes that she is Mrs Heathcliff. In *The Tenant of Wildfell Hall* (hereafter referred to as *Wildfell Hall*) the narrative is also framed by a male character, Gilbert Markham, who at one point

Wuthering Heights and *Wildfell Hall* contain narratives within narratives.

spectacularly misjudges the situation, assaulting Helen's brother as a rival suitor. Helen tells her own story through the diary which she gives him to read. Most of Charlotte's novels feature a first-person narrator. While there is less likelihood of confusion here, we must remember that narrators can be unreliable.

SETTINGS

In reading any Brontë novel, it is helpful to note settings and their symbolism. In *Wuthering Heights* there is a simple division: Wuthering Heights represents nature in the raw; Thrushcross Grange stands for culture and the civilized Establishment. In *Jane Eyre* the action occurs in five main settings, in each of which Jane learns something new. Moreover the name of each is a useful clue: Gateshead – the start of her journey; Lowood – a place of dark threat; Thornfield – trial and tribulation; Marsh End – escape from a moral quagmire; and Ferndean – a secluded haven. A similar significance is found, for example, in Wildfell Hall, whose isolation and neglect echo the state of its occupant.

A SENSE OF DRAMA

All three sisters possess a great sense of drama and an ability to stage-manage individual scenes. Perhaps this stems from the plays they wrote and performed together as children. The influence of Shakespeare may also be a factor. Certainly one of his dramatic motifs, the love triangle, features strongly in their work, as it does in the representative scenes discussed below. All three, in their different ways, are adept at dialogue.

WUTHERING HEIGHTS

In the famous deathbed scene of *Wuthering Heights* (Ch. 15), Emily portrays elemental passions. Heathcliff has entered the Grange through an open door in order to see Cathy. Look out for doors, windows and walls in this novel: they represent thresholds between worlds, possibilities, or freedom and constraint. Heathcliff embraces his soulmate Cathy, who is now married to, and pregnant by, Edgar Linton.

Heathcliff's eyes burn with anguish (suggesting passion and hellfire). Heathcliff and Catherine speak with characteristic directness:

> 'I wish I could hold you,' she continued, bitterly, 'till we were both dead! I shouldn't care what you suffered. I care nothing for your sufferings. Why shouldn't you suffer? I do!'

She torments him with bitter speculation about what he will say after she has died. Nelly's allusion to heaven as 'a land of exile' to Catherine, Heathcliff's savage question, 'Are you possessed with a devil … to talk in that manner to me when you are dying?', and his reference to her 'infernal selfishness' and of how he will 'writhe in torments of hell' all point to the novel's mythical core. This reverses the biblical Fall: Heathcliff is associated with Satan, and Wuthering Heights with hell; yet Catherine, a child of nature, 'falls' from natural grace when she chooses Edgar and culture instead of Heathcliff.

In a passionate climax, Catherine springs into Heathcliff's arms. Heathcliff gnashes his teeth at Nelly and foams 'like a mad dog' – again linking him to the animal world. His anguished 'would you like to live with your soul in the grave?' reveals that he and Catherine are aspects of the psyche, not merely human characters. So skilfully is the scene managed, with its narration by down-to-earth Nelly, that even Catherine's final 'I shall die! I shall die!' transcends melodrama.

THE TENANT OF WILDFELL HALL

Anne, typically, paints a more restrained and Christian climactic scene in Chapter 23 of *Wildfell Hall*. This also deals with a 'fall' from innocence, and appropriately it takes place at night in an autumnal garden. Helen Huntingdon has refused to admit that her husband Arthur is a hopelessly depraved and egotistical womanizer. In a moment of poignant **dramatic irony** she finds him alone in the shrubbery, clasps him affectionately from

KEYWORD

Dramatic irony: when the reader (or audience) is aware of an important fact of which one character is unaware.

behind, and fails to understand that his 'Bless you, darling' is meant for another woman. A little later, Hargrave, who has designs on Helen, beats her at chess – symbolizing his desire to entrap her. Dark hints force Helen to suspect her husband at last, and she revisits the garden in time to hear him proclaim his love to Annabella. Helen's biblical language, alluding to the book of Job, points to her sense of being beset by trials. The tree which shelters her suggests the Cross, and it is the Christian God on whom she calls – in contrast to Catherine and Heathcliff. The answering 'heavenly influence', however, communicates itself through the natural world of stars, wind and moon.

JANE EYRE

A major turning point in *Jane Eyre* occurs in Chapter 23, in the garden of Thornfield at midsummer eve. After a painterly description of a majestic sunset, the narrator Jane walks in the garden after her work is done. A telltale whiff of Rochester's cigar smoke makes her retreat to the orchard. A rising moon, as so often in Charlotte's work, hints at the presence of the **mother goddess**. The richly lyrical description of the 'antique garden', its flowers making their 'evening sacrifice of incense',

> **KEYWORDS**
>
> **Mother goddess:** in pagan religion, a goddess representing nature as a mother.
>
> **Metaphor:** an image (word picture) in which something is spoken of as if it were something essentially different but in some way similar.

evokes a sense of Eden-like natural divinity. This is intensified by a shift into the present tense: 'I look round and listen. I see trees laden with ripening fruit. I hear a nightingale …'

The conversation between Rochester and Jane perfectly conveys both their familiarity and their unequal social status (another shared Brontë theme). Characteristically, Rochester's talk of his impending marriage to Blanche Ingram is a trick, since he wants to marry Jane. In fact he has already tricked Blanche into revealing that she did not really love him. And though Jane does not know it, his later words, 'It will atone – it will atone', allude to an even greater deception: he has a mad wife hidden in the attic! Jane's passionate insistence on her spiritual equality – 'I have as much soul as you – and full as much heart!' – eloquently embodies the sentiments of all three sisters.

Charlotte's remarkable use of symbolism and **metaphor** repay close attention. In this scene, there are the symbols of the garden and the nightingale, and Rochester's image of Jane as 'a wild frantic bird that is rending its own plumage in its desperation'. An exotic moth hints at Rochester's secret West Indian marriage. However, the key image is the horse chestnut tree writhing and groaning in the pre-storm wind, and then split by lightning. At one level this is Gothic Romance, but at another it symbolizes divine disapproval, Rochester's moral equivocation, Jane's dual nature – reason and passion, and the lovers' coming separation.

✳ ✳ ✳ SUMMARY ✳ ✳ ✳

● Anne is good at succinct character profiles; Emily's characters are mythic; Charlotte's are psyschologically profound.

● Consider the significance of names and settings.

● Remain aware of narrative viewpoint – who is telling the story.

● Look out especially for Emily's symbolism, Anne's handling of dramatic scenes and Charlotte's use of setting to create atmosphere.

3 Biography and Influences

Elizabeth Gaskell began a 'Brontë myth' by blaming the sisters' upbringing for what some critics saw as the unladylike 'coarseness' of their novels. Many writers have followed her lead in interpreting the novels in terms of the sisters' own experiences. These experiences were certainly formative, yet they should be considered alongside wider social and literary influences.

WOMEN'S RIGHTS

The sisters were keenly aware of the restraints on women in the male-dominated society in which they lived. It has been said that feminism began with *A Vindication of the Rights of Woman*, by Mary Wollstonecraft, in 1792. Its sentiments are certainly shared by Charlotte's Jane Eyre when she insists that 'women feel just as men feel; they need exercise for their faculties, and a field for their efforts as much as their brothers do' (*Jane Eyre*, Ch. 12).

Upper- and middle-class women were supposed to be decorative, and accomplished in genteel arts that would please their husbands; they were not educated for careers. They had no political power and, if married, no legal rights. Hence in both *Wuthering Heights* and *Wildfell Hall* men refer to, and treat, their wives as their property. Women could not obtain a divorce until 1857 (the year of Charlotte's death), and until 1870 everything a woman owned became her husband's property.

The plight of single women also became more acute in the mid-nineteenth century as their numbers increased owing to a higher male infant mortality rate, emigration and men marrying later. Single women such as Anne's Agnes Grey and Charlotte's Jane Eyre had two career options: to become teachers or governesses.

THE FAMILY BACKGROUND

Patrick Brontë (né Brunty) came from a poor family in northern Ireland but, against the odds, achieved a place at Cambridge University and then obtained a curacy in Hartshead, Yorkshire. He was an Anglican. His wife Maria, whom he married in 1812, came from a Wesleyan Methodist Cornish family. Six children were born in eight years: Maria (1813), Elizabeth (1815), Charlotte (1816), Branwell (1817), Emily (1818) and Anne (1820). In 1819 the family moved to Haworth, a high and rather bleak industrial village on the edge of the moors, on which the children rambled. Emily's love for the moors appears in *Wuthering Heights*, which Charlotte calls 'moorish, and wild, and knotty as the root of heath'. However, the sisters' awareness of industrial life is shown in Charlotte's novels *The Professor* and *Shirley*.

Life was generally hard, and serious illness common, especially the tuberculosis that decimated the Brontës. (The 1850 Babbage Report reveals that in Haworth 41.6 per cent of children died before the age of six.) Neither were the children sheltered from contemporary issues. Luddite riots had occurred locally within living memory. Workers were exploited, and poverty was rife. The children heard about social problems from their father and to some extent witnessed them at first hand. Gaskell describes Haworth's 'wild, rough population':

> Their accost is curt; their accent and tone of speech blunt and harsh. …
> They have a quick perception of character, and a keen sense of humour;
> the dwellers among them must be prepared for certain
> uncomplimentary, though most likely true, observations, pithily
> expressed. Their feelings are not easily roused, but their duration is
> lasting.
>
> (Gaskell, *The Life of Charlotte Brontë*, 1996)

Readers of *Wuthering Heights* will see some of its characters in this description. The perceptiveness and outspokenness can be observed in *The Professor* in the character of Hunsden. Gaskell goes on to say that the local men 'are sleuth-hounds in pursuit of money' – like mill owner Edward Crimsworth in the same novel.

Family influence was, however, probably stronger than that of the locality. The eldest girl, Maria, was aged 7 when the children's mother died. Their Aunt Branwell, Patrick's sister-in-law, came to keep house. Anne, the youngest, shared a bed with her and formed a stronger bond with her than did the others, absorbing more of her Methodism. Anne's religious feelings inspired *Wildfell Hall*. The loss of their mother strongly affected all three sisters, notwithstanding Anne's relationship with her aunt. Almost every Brontë novel has a motherless main character, and this is a particular feature of Charlotte's work.

Their father was an intelligent man of strong opinions who discussed current affairs with his children, read them newspapers and encouraged them to read. In addition, Maria read them accounts of parliamentary debates. The children grew up disputing the merits of great leaders such as Wellington (Charlotte's idol). Gaskell's claims that Patrick cut up a dress of his wife's, burned his children's boots, angrily sawed the legs off furniture and daily fired a pistol to discharge his anger are almost certainly exaggerated. He may have been a rather daunting figure, and yet it seems he was in his way a caring and supportive father. There is probably something of him in Charlotte's portrayal of Monsieur Paul in *Villette* and Anne's Reverend Millward in *Wildfell Hall*.

SCHOOL AND JUVENILIA

In 1824 Patrick sent the four eldest girls to the Reverend Wilson's School for Clergymen's Daughters at Cowan Bridge. Parents paid £14 a year for a girl's board and lodging, while the education itself was paid for by charity. The establishment taught 'history, geography, the use of the globes, grammar, writing and arithmetic, all kinds of needlework, and the nicer kinds of household work'. Yet it was poorly administered, spartan, cold and damp, and the diet extremely poor. Emphasis was placed on humbling the girls by impressing on them their lowly position and debt to society. Mrs Gaskell describes a Miss Scatcherd's cruel injustice to the sick Maria. Miss Temple was a more sympathetic teacher, who nonetheless counselled quiet endurance.

Weakened by this regime, Maria and Elizabeth died from tuberculosis a few months apart from each other in 1825 – a great loss to the family, and one which later found its way into *Jane Eyre*. The gentle Maria was to become the model for the consumptive Helen Burns in *Jane Eyre*, the Reverend Wilson for Brocklehurst and Miss Temple for a character of the same name. Shocked at the deaths of his two eldest daughters, and by reports of food contamination, Patrick Brontë took Charlotte and Emily away from the school after a term.

United in loss, the surviving children created intense imaginary worlds. When Charlotte was aged about 10 they began to write precocious stories and poems about these worlds, creating tiny books with almost unreadably small handwritten text. Branwell and Charlotte created the Glasstown Confederacy, and then Angria. Emily and Anne dreamed up Gondal. These literary worlds matured over several years, and from the last eventually came some of Emily's finest poems.

In 1831 the 15-year-old Charlotte was sent to Roe Head, a gentler school run by Margaret Wooler. Here Charlotte made two lifelong friends, Ellen Nussey and Mary Taylor. But Patrick could only afford for her to stay for a year and a half, after which she came home to pass on what she had learned to her siblings. She described this at the time as a 'delightful, though somewhat monotonous' phase of her life.

In 1835 she returned to Roe Head as a teacher. Emily accompanied her as a pupil but returned home after only two months, apparently almost dying of homesickness for the moors. She was replaced by Anne.

THE BLACK SHEEP

In such a prodigiously talented family it is easy to dismiss Branwell as an underachiever. However, he played an essential role in the creative hothouse that led to the flowering of his sisters' work. It is hard to

Perhaps too much was expected of Branwell.

evaluate the level of his own native talent, but it seems likely that he suffered under the strain of what was expected of him by his family. Admittedly, he had a high opinion of his own talents, although, like Charlotte, not of his appearance. (He was small, with red hair and sharp features, and often drew caricatures of himself.) In 1836 he tried to persuade *Blackwood's Magazine* to sack one of its major contributors and hire him instead. He also wrote to Wordsworth, flattering the great poet yet recommending himself in unfortunate terms: 'Surely in this day when there is not a *writing* poet worth a sixpence the field must be open if a better man can step forward.'

Failing in this enterprise, Branwell managed to secure some portrait commissions, but by 1839 he was drinking heavily, and in 1840 he lost a post as tutor. He was sacked from the post of railway clerk for accounting 'irregularities'. His last chance came when he became a tutor at Thorp Green, where Anne was a governess. After a year and a half, however, he was dismissed for having an affair with the lady of the house, Mrs Lydia Robinson, 17 years his senior. In a letter addressed in an erratic hand to his friend Francis Grundy, Branwell gives his version of how the affair began, fired by his admiration for Mrs Robinson, her warm response and his distress at 'the heartless and unmanly manner in which she was treated by an eunuch like fellow [her husband] who though possessed of such a treasure never even occupied the same apartment with her' (letter formerly in author's possession).

In 1846 her husband died, but Branwell's hope that she would marry him was dashed. Disappointed, Branwell sank into an alcoholic and opiated decline, attended by his long-suffering sisters. His affair at Thorp Green, followed by his sickbed ravings and self-pity, probably inspired Anne's portrayal of Huntingdon in *Wildfell Hall*, and some of the scenes in *Wuthering Heights*. Branwell died in 1848.

BRUSSELS

In early 1842, funded by Aunt Branwell, Charlotte and Emily set off for Brussels to study and work at the Pensionnat Heger. Its principal, Constantin Heger, was an intense, forceful and irascible man. He rated Emily's intellect more highly than Charlotte's, but liked the latter more because she was more tractable. Indeed, Charlotte became dependent on him emotionally. The two girls were taken on for another six months as au pairs, but this was interrupted by the death of their Aunt Branwell.

After the funeral, Charlotte returned to the Pensionnat to teach. Shy and frail, she was never suited to teaching. Added to this, she fell in love with Heger. His wife, meanwhile, was determined to forestall any romantic connection. Charlotte came home in misery less than a year later. Despite this, the whole Brussels experience was artistically formative for her. Heger was the model for Monsier Paul in *Villette* (Charlotte's name for Brussels), his wife for Madame Beck. The account of Lucy Snowe's visit to a Roman Catholic confessional is taken from this time. *The Professor* is also based closely on Charlotte's Brussels experience, although its protagonist is a man.

LITERARY INFLUENCES

The Brontë children read widely, especially the novels of Walter Scott, and much poetry. In 1834 Charlotte recommended to a friend: 'Milton, Shakespeare, Thomson, Goldsmith, Pope (if you will, though I don't admire him), Scott, Byron, Campbell, Wordsworth, and Southey'. Milton and Shakespeare are evident in the cosmology and the plot of *Wuthering Heights*, and in the creation of Hareton, who resembles Caliban in *The Tempest* (see page 36).

KEYWORDS

Romantics: the followers of a movement in the arts which reacted to the rationalist Age of Enlightenment and the Industrial Revolution. The movement emphasized the freedom of the individual, the power of nature, equality and the irrational.

Byron is a key figure, epitomizing the wild, dark, individualistic heroes beloved of the **Romantics**. Heathcliff and Rochester are Byronic heroes. In a sense, so too is Jane Eyre.

It should also be stressed that the Brontë sisters had a powerful interaction with each other. Their regular habit was to stay up discussing their work in progress after their father had gone to bed, and of course they read each other's work. More than this, there is something special in the cross-fertilizing creative power of three sisters, like the triple goddesses of their Celtic ancestors, that made them greater than the sum of their parts.

A more direct kind of influence is seen in *Wildfell Hall*, which was Anne's morally upright reply to the alcoholism, violence and injustice presented so amorally in *Wuthering Heights*. Branwell was more of an influence on his sisters by the manner of his decline and death than by his rather mediocre adult writings.

One pragmatic influence on the sisters was the need to earn a living. The poet Southey had written to the aspiring Charlotte in 1837: 'Literature cannot be the business of a woman's life, and it ought not to be.' Yet the school that Charlotte and Emily tried to start had received not one pupil. A book of the sisters' poems published in 1846 eventually sold a total of six copies. There had been, however, some commercially successful women novelists. Jane Austen is the prime example, although the sisters did not read her. (When Charlotte did, she was unimpressed.) By the middle of the century there was a large market for novels, so writing them was a reasonable career choice for three sisters ill qualified for other occupations.

* * * SUMMARY * * *

- Women's rights were a major concern for all three sisters.

- Reverend Patrick Brontë was Irish, his wife Cornish. There were six children. When their mother died they were looked after by their aunt. They lived in Haworth, Yorkshire.

- The four eldest girls went to Cowan Bridge school. Maria and Elizabeth died from the conditions there. Charlotte was happier at Roe Head school.

- The children wrote tiny books about imaginary worlds: Gondal and Angria.

- Branwell was the 'black sheep' of the family. He died of an alcohol-related illness.

- Charlotte and Emily went to Brussels to study.

- They were especially influenced by Scott, Shakespeare and Byron.

4 Major Themes

A ROLE FOR WOMEN

The Brontë sisters' own situation compelled them to earn a living, and as motherless daughters there was a special sense in which they had to forge their own identities. Opposed to all this was the Victorian view of the ideal woman: meek, gentle, respectful, calm, delicate and never overtly sexual. The ideal woman married and had children; she did not pursue a career. The poet Southey reflected the prevailing view when he counselled Charlotte against ambition and a desire for fame.

Anne Brontë was the most pious of the sisters, but she by no means upheld the sexual status quo. For Helen, the heroine of *Wildfell Hall*, work as a fee-earning artist is both practically and psychologically vital to her independence and self-respect. Through her, the author expresses strong opinions about the moral equality of women, arguing that girls should be given the same freedom as boys, not 'taught to cling to others for direction and support, and guarded, as much as possible, from the very knowledge of evil' (Ch. 3).

Charlotte also insists on equality, although rather ambivalently. Her heroines all form relationships with older men who dominate them yet are attracted to them precisely because these women dare to assert themselves as equals. For these young women, their male heroes are instructors and initiators, not least in a sexual sense. Despite this apparent attraction to dominant men, Charlotte also stresses the importance of gainful employment. The need to earn money is what launches both Jane Eyre and Lucy Snowe on their journeys of self-discovery. Near the end of *Villette*, Lucy Snowe is overjoyed when Paul Emmanuel sets her up in her own school. In *Shirley* the older man is Robert Moore, and his young admirer Caroline Helstone. She complains to him that she is 'not quite satisfied' because she is 'making no money', wishing that she were a boy and could become his apprentice (Ch. 5). Later, when she thinks she will never marry, she confronts a bleak future:

> I have to live, perhaps, till seventy years. As far as I know, I have good health; half a century of existence may lie before me. How am I to occupy it? What am I to do to fill the interval of time which spreads between me and the grave?'

(Ch. 10)

The world of *Wuthering Heights* is even more restricted. Here, women only become wives or servants. Yet Catherine Earnshaw never bows to male dominance. Even when her dying father asks her, 'Why canst thou not always be a good lass, Cathy?', she laughingly replies: 'Why can you not always be a good man, father?' (Ch. 5). Young Cathy finds a role for herself in polishing a rough diamond, Hareton Earnshaw, which is not altogether unlike the role that Helen initially sets herself in *Wildfell Hall*.

The question of female purpose is addressed most fully in *Villette*. We encounter it, for example, in Chapter 14 when Paul Emmanuel bullies Lucy Snowe into taking a role in the school play. The question arises more explicitly in Chapter 19 when Lucy goes to an art gallery and sees paintings representing male stereoptypes of the female role. Charlotte, in the voice of Lucy, is predictably scornful.

POWER AND IMPRISONMENT

The Brontës grew up in a society in which oppression was commonplace. There is a story of Emily establishing mastery over her bull mastiff dog, dragging it downstairs while beating it over the nose with her free hand – and then tending its wounds herself. *Wuthering Heights* is full of this kind of raw power struggle, often on a physical level. When Heathcliff first comes to the Heights as an orphaned waif, he is bullied by Hindley, but gradually learns how to capitalize on being old Earnshaw's favourite. When Earnshaw dies, Heathcliff is beaten and degraded by Hindley. For this, Heathcliff later takes a calculated revenge.

In Brontë novels most relationships involve power struggles.

Possessing a nature brutally indifferent to sympathetic appeals, Heathcliff himself becomes an arch-oppressor. He cynically marries and then abuses and imprisons Isabella; he tyrannizes his puny son Linton; he kidnaps and imprisons Nelly and young Cathy, forcing the latter to marry Linton; and he keeps Hareton in a prison of ignorance from which he is only released by young Cathy's instruction. Even the weather can be imprisoning, as Lockwood finds when he is snowbound at the Heights (Ch. 2).

Helen, in *Wildfell Hall*, becomes a virtual prisoner when her husband discovers her plan to leave him. He confiscates her keys and money, and with disempowering cruelty burns the painting materials with which she had hoped to make a living, and destroys her paintings. Imprisonment is also a feature in both *Jane Eyre* and *Villette*. In a richly symbolic scene in Chapter 2 of the former, the young Jane, rebelling against her cousin's bullying, is marched off and shut in the red-room. The servants are on the verge of using their garters to restrain her, a detail which Elaine Showalter relates to Victorian erotic fantasies of containment and corporal punishment (Showalter, *A Literature of Their Own*, 1978, pp. 115–16).

This highlights a feature of these fantasies, and of patriarchal oppression in Charlotte's novels: namely, that women often act as the gaolers of women. In *Jane Eyre*, the saintly Helen Burns is bullied and flogged by Miss Scatcherd, acting on behalf of that great pillar of patriarchy, Brocklehurst. Rochester's mad wife has as gaoler the menacing Grace Poole. Madame Beck in *Villette* is in a sense Lucy's gaoler, taking impressions of her keys in order to pry into her private possessions.

However, the strongest image of imprisonment is of women locked in attics: mad Bertha Mason (in reality Bertha Rochester) in *Jane Eyre*, and *Villette*'s Lucy Snowe, who is locked in the attic by Paul Emmanuel to learn her lines for the school play – or in symbolic terms to learn to play the role forced on her by male-dominated society. The attic becomes a symbol for the unconscious, in which is locked away all that women are forced to repress – especially their rage.

Another feature of imprisonment in Brontë novels is that when women are locked away, literally or symbolically, they starve. After several hours in the attic, Lucy is famished. The girls in the 'prison' school of Jane Eyre's Lowood are constantly undernourished. Jane is nearly starving when she reaches the relative freedom of Marsh End and the Rivers family. Isabella cannot stomach the rough diet at Wuthering Heights, and has to go hungry. Most powerfully, Catherine Earnshaw's decision to starve herself – employing the traditional weapon of the oppressed, the hunger strike – helps to kill her. (It has been suggested that anorexia is the sufferer's attempt to exercise autonomy.) In a restrictive patriarchal society, women are mentally and emotionally undernourished.

On a level that transcends gender politics, imprisonment for the Brontës stands for the imprisonment of the soul in its earthly form.

This is most explicit in Emily's poetry, and to a lesser extent in Anne's. Emily, for example, in 'High waving heather, 'neath stormy blasts bending', rejoices in a night in the open:

> Earth rising to heaven and heaven descending,
> Man's spirit away from its drear dungeon sending,
> Bursting the fetters and breaking the bars.

There are also more 'sociological' portrayals of power and class in some Brontë novels. Notably, we find the rich but repellent Edward Crimsworth in *The Professor*, theatening to whip his impoverished brother. There is also Charlotte's *Shirley*, in which she portrays the clash of interests that led to the Luddite riots. In its appraisal of social issues the novel resembles Gaskell's *North and South*. Both novels portray the wretched plight of the unemployed, but reject violence and argue for philanthropic compromise rather than socialist solutions. There is also an element of class struggle and oppression in *Wuthering Heights*. We may imagine that the world of Thrushcross Grange is powerless and effete, but in fact its power is that of the Establishment. Edgar may not be physically Heathcliff's equal, but he is a magistrate and can call on servants to act as his 'muscle'.

LOVE AND MARRIAGE

The Brontë girls had little direct experience of romantic love. Through their father they met local curates (satirized in *Shirley*). In particular, Patrick's assistant William Weightman, handsome, charming and flirtatious, is credited with having aroused their amorous feelings. Charlotte, of course, fell in love with her domineering mentor Monsieur Heger, and was rebuffed. Anne observed a more carnal love at relatively close quarters in Branwell's affair with Mrs Robinson at Thorp Park. For home-centred and retiring Emily, love was – as far as we know – merely an elevated idea.

Emily's lack of experience shows in *Wuthering Heights*, which is often regarded as, above all, a great love story but is no model for real life.

The love between Catherine and Heathcliff exists on some craggy mountain peak raised above ordinary human romance – and above mere marriage. When Nelly questions Catherine regarding her proposed marriage to Edgar Linton, Catherine scorns the idea that it will separate her from Heathcliff: 'My love for Linton is like the foliage in the woods. Time will change it, I'm well aware, as winter changes the trees – my love for Heathcliff resembles the eternal rocks beneath – a source of little visible delight, but necessary' (Ch. 9).

Their love seems to survive the grave. Not only does Heathcliff, in a grisly taboo-breaking (and very Gothic) scene, dig up and embrace Catherine's corpse, but he is also haunted by her after her death, and goes to his own death sublimely transported by the prospect of reunion with her. Emily's poems occasionally speak of love but, as one might expect from that of Heathcliff and Catherine, the beloved is always dead and, therefore, safely beyond the tarnishing influence of everyday life.

In the Brontë novels, a dance of power goes on before love can be fulfilled. *Wuthering Heights* ends on a note of romantic promise not just because Heathcliff is dead, but because Hareton bows to Catherine Linton's power to civilize him. In *Jane Eyre*, Rochester is attracted to Jane because she scorns subservience, declaring: 'it is my spirit that addresses your spirit; just as if both had passed through the grave, and we stood at God's feet, equal – as we are!' (Ch. 23). Significantly, this is the prelude to the moment of high romance when he proposes to her: 'enclosing me in his arms, gathering me to his breast, pressing his lips to my lips'. This is the stuff of swooning heroines, but the language speaks subtly of domination. Soon he is calling her his 'mustard-seed', 'little sunny-faced … girl-bride', joking about keeping her on a chain and alluding to Turkish harems. When he showers her with expensive dresses of his choice, she is uncomfortable, sensing that he is beginning to make her his possession. As narrator, she jokes uneasily that she is becoming 'one Jane Rochester, a person whom as yet I knew not'.

(Compare this with the discovery in Hardy's *Far from the Madding Crowd* that Boldwood has a cupboard full of clothes labelled 'Bathsheba Boldwood'.) Sadly, it is only when Rochester has literally 'been through the fire', and lost his eyesight and a hand, that he is sufficiently humbled truly to love Jane as an equal, and to respect her own identity. The fact that Jane has in the interval inherited the modern-day equivalent of £1 million probably helps too!

Charlotte wrote *Villette* partly to try to come to terms with the lack of love in her own life, and with her doomed love for Heger. In response to Harriet Martineau's criticism that its female characters think only of love, Gilbert and Gubar assert: 'that is precisely Brontë's point' (Gilbert and Gubar, 1979, p. 407): romantic love is almost the sole opportunity for personal fulfilment that these characters have, but it clashes with their need for autonomy. Ice-maidenly Lucy Snowe begins to thaw in the presence of the upright Dr John, 'the best gentleman in Christendom' (Ch. 13). Characterizing herself as 'loverless and inexpectant of love' and resigning herself to the 'heart-poverty' that she assumes goes with being poor, plain and small (like Jane Eyre and Charlotte herself), she nevertheless falls in love with Dr John. As a friend, she disabuses him of his infatuation with Ginevra Fanshawe, and smoothes the path of his budding romance with the more suitable Polly, but all the time he remains obtusely unaware of Lucy's feelings for him. Alone in the attic, she devours his friendly letters, drawing sustenance from them in secret. Eventually, in an act powerfully symbolizing her self-denial, she buries them in the garden.

The development of Lucy's relationship with Paul Emmanuel is characterized by a constant power struggle, beginning with the espisode in which he locks her in the attic to learn the part he has made her take on. Like Jane Eyre with Rochester, Lucy has to struggle to be taken seriously. Monsieur Paul suspiciously resents her intelligence: 'He believed in his soul that lovely, placid, and passive feminine mediocrity was the only pillow on which manly thought and sense could find rest for its aching temples; and as to work, male mind alone could work to any good practical result' (Ch. 30).

Even allowing the standards of the time, and Paul's penchant for provocation, this is fairly sexist! He softens when he thinks she is about to admit herself an ignoramus, then bristles again when she insists on having some knowledge of her own. The love that develops between the apparently ill-matched pair is based on a slowly developing mutual respect and friendship.

OUTSIDERS AND ORIGINS

The typical Brontë hero or heroine is a social outsider. Often they are orphaned, or at least motherless (like the Brontë children). In part the outsider role is a function of narrative technique, since a first-person narrative can most easily be related by someone only marginally involved in what is described. Lockwood in *Wuthering Heights* is the classic case, since he never becomes very involved in the story being told. Heathcliff is from the start an outsider who embodies the mystery of origin. No one knows his background; he is a foundling, a cuckoo in the nest.

Helen in *Wildfell Hall* becomes an outsider when she flees her husband and has to conceal her identity, although her slightly austere nature also distances her from others. Charlotte's Jane Eyre and Lucy Snowe have much in common as outsiders: both, like Charlotte, 'little and plain' and pessimistic about their marriage prospects. Both are poor and obliged to take jobs which set them apart from ordinary society, far away from their homes – if indeed they can be said to have homes. Both find solace in the moon, an obvious mother symbol. Both are naturally retiring and rather sceptical about society. The alienated narrator of *The Professor*, William Crimsworth, is similarly lacking in social skills, while Robert Moore in *Shirley* is not only a foreigner, but one who alienates local workers by replacing them with machines in his mill.

For all these outsiders, the journey through life is about coming home – about finding a sense of belonging, if not in society then in the love of another.

DEATH, DREAMS AND THE SUPERNATURAL

The Brontë children listened to local ghost stories, lived next to an overfilled graveyard in an era of high mortality and in a village with an even higher mortality rate than those nearby, and shared the Victorian preoccupation with death. Dreams, which came in the 'counterfeit death' of sleep, were just beginning to be regarded as psychological indicators rather than as either prophetic or mere nonsense. Thus in the Brontë novels and poems, death, dreams and the supernatural abound.

Wuthering Heights begins with three of its main characters already dead: Hindley, Catherine and Edgar. Their story is told posthumously by the housekeeper, Nelly. Death, dreams and the supernatural are quickly combined in the remarkable scene in the second chapter in which Lockwood is obliged to sleep in a coffin-like oak closet in Catherine Earnshaw's old room. Lockwood's first dream is partly a confused reworking of the day's events, though it also refers to his sense of being under attack in the Heights. The second dream is of a different order. Attempting to silence a knocking at the window, he dashes his hand through the pane (symbolizing the veil between this world and the next) and finds his fingers closed 'on the fingers of a little, ice-cold hand'. 'Let me in – let me in!' cries the shivering voice of Catherine.

In the later narration, the living Catherine describes how in a dream that reminds us of William Blake's unconventional views, she died and found herself in heaven, but was unhappy there: 'heaven did not seem to be my home, and I broke my heart with weeping to come back to earth; and the angels were so angry that they flung me out into the middle of the heath on the top of Wuthering Heights, where I woke sobbing for joy' (Ch. 9).

For Emily, death represents an escape from the prison of life. Nearing death, Catherine confides in Nelly: 'the thing that irks me most is this shattered prison, after all. I'm tired, tired of being enclosed here. I'm wearying to escape into that glorious world, and to be always there'.

For Charlotte, always torn between Reason and Imagination (as personified in *Villette*), dreams are prophetic or psychologically significant, but the apparently supernatural usually turns out to have a down-to-earth explanation. Jane Eyre's dream of herself 'following the windings of an unknown road', carrying a wailing baby, with Rochester disappearing into the night before her foreshadows the confusion to come, through which she must nurture her own orphaned 'inner child'. When she next sees a horrifying figure reminding her of 'the foul German spectre – the vampire', trying on her wedding veil and then rending it in two, she passes out in terror for the second time in her life – the first being as a child in the red-room when she thought she saw her uncle's ghost. This new 'spectre' turns out to be Bertha, Rochester's mad wife, on a midnight ramble.

In *Villette*, a ghostly nun who is supposed to have been buried alive in the garden turns out to be de Hamal, Ginevra Fanshawe's foppish lover using this disguise to gain access to his beloved. At the same time, the nun is a powerful symbol, representing the passionate side of Lucy's nature, also 'buried alive'.

RELIGION
It is hardly surprising that the novels of a clergyman's daughters should be full of religious references. Emily was the least conventional in her spiritual outlook. Her religion seems to be very personal. To her, hell is as much here on earth as anywhere else. Heathcliff is frequently referred to as 'infernal' and a 'devil'. Conventional Christianity is represented by the punitive, flesh-mortifying pronouncements of the old servant Joseph.

For much of Anne's short life she agonized about the Calvinist doctrine of the Elect, which holds that only a select band of followers were destined for heaven. In *Wildfell Hall*, Helen consoles herself with the thought that her reprobate husband will eventually be saved by God's grace. Anne expresses a similar sentiment in her poem 'A Word to the Elect': 'That as in Adam all have died,/ In Christ shall all men live.' She also castigates the self-satisfaction of those who believe themselves to be among 'the chosen'.

Charlotte often alludes to the Bible to illustrate a point. To the educated Victorian reader, it was a shared reference point. In *Agnes Grey*, Anne criticizes the worldly and self-satisfied career clergyman, comparing him with the genuinely Christian variety. Nor does Charlotte afford automatic respect to 'men of the cloth', as is shown by the satirical way in which she presents those who have no real calling in *Shirley*. The tone is set by the wry opening, in which she refers to 'an abundant shower of curates' who 'ought to be doing a great deal of good'. Here, 'ought' is the operative word! In similar vein, Helstone is portrayed as a man who should have been a soldier rather than a rector. However, Charlotte reserves her real contempt for Catholicism, which to her mind encouraged an abandonment of personal responsibility. Lucy Snowe's narrative in *Villette* is peppered with anti-Catholic jibes accusing Catholics of superstition and dishonesty. This sentiment mingles with Charlotte's patriotism and xenophobia: Lucy's pupils are seen to be not just stupid and lazy compared with English girls, but sneaky. Lucy is tempted by Catholicism only when on the verge of a breakdown.

CHILDHOOD AND EDUCATION

The Brontës explore childhood as no other Victorian novelist does, with the possible exception of Dickens. They frequently write about cruelty to, and by, children and about how the corruption of children by adults can blight their character. In *Wildfell Hall*, Helen blames Huntingdon's bad character on his parenting. We also see his determination to make his son copy his own bad behaviour. Having removed her son from this bad influence, Helen uses aversion therapy to make little Arthur hate the taste of alcohol.

In *Wuthering Heights* cruelty to children is routine. Most obvious is Heathcliff's degradation of Hareton in revenge for his own. Emily's attitude towards education seems ambivalent. Heathcliff is degraded partly by being denied education, yet the shallow Lockwood is no advertisement for it, and educated Edgar's retreat to his library after his wife's death is portrayed as a retreat from reality. Joseph uses Bible readings to chastize the children and to confirm his own prejudices. Hareton begins to discover a 'brave new world' when he learns to read, but at the expense of his autonomy.

Jane Eyre vividly portrays Jane's cruel treatment at the hands of the 14-year-old John Reed and his mother, and of Brocklehurst. Education is seen as a largely negative influence at Lowood, but as a positive one when Jane herself becomes a tutor and then a schoolmistress. Education plays a more important role in *Villette* and *The Professor*, but in both novels Charlotte focuses more on the power struggle involved in controlling pupils than on questions of what, and how, they learn.

✸ ✸ ✸ SUMMARY ✸ ✸ ✸

Some of the Brontës' main themes are:

● The search for a fulfilling role for women, equal to that of men.

● Power and imprisonment, especially the oppression of women by men.

● Love and marriage, both of which can be seen as fulfilling or destructive.

● Death, dreams and the supernatural, often linked to the Gothic genre.

● Religion, including Anne's resistance to Calvinism, Charlotte's concern with moral responsibility and Emily's paganism.

● Childhood and education, and cruelty to, and by, children.

5 Major Works

WUTHERING HEIGHTS

Emily's startlingly original novel was published under the name of Ellis Bell in 1847, a year before she died.

Framed narrative

One mark of the novel's genius is its innovative structure, in which the narrative is framed by an 'unreliable' male narrator, Lockwood, and swings between two main settings. Nelly is the 'human fixture' (Lockwood's term) who knits it all together. Most of the story is told in flashbacks, emphasizing how the present emerges from the past. Thus the novel begins near the story's end, at a point of stagnation; resolution only comes after the final flashback. Added to this is a fugue-like circularity: history repeats itself, but with significant variations. Heathcliff begins to see his own youthful self in Hareton, and is painfully reminded of Catherine in her daughter. But whereas the love between Heathcliff and Catherine is destructive, that between Hareton and young Cathy brings hope.

The narrative style owes something to the technique used by Mary Shelley in *Frankenstein*: we are given 'evidence' to interpret, discovering information piece by piece, as does Lockwood. This anticipates modern novelists such as A.S. Byatt and Ian McEwan. Another 'modern' feature is the way in which the separate narrators within Nelly's narrative – Heathcliff, both Catherines, Isabella and Zillah – provide different perspectives, always in character. We are even led to question Nelly's reliability as a narrator. The author herself remains enigmatic throughout. Jane Eyre *is* Charlotte, but Nelly Dean is *not* Emily. There is no direct authorial commentary: Emily's characters speak for themselves.

What kind of novel is it?

Is *Wuthering Heights* an attempt at realism, or a mythic psychodrama in which the characters represent elemental or psychic forces? Certainly it is realistic in physical details, for example when Lockwood describes Heathcliff's wind-buffeted residence: 'Happily, the architect had foresight to build it strong; the narrow windows are deeply set in the wall, and the corners defended with large jutting stones' (Ch. 1). Inside, similar attention is given to 'ranks of immense pewter dishes, interspersed with silver jugs and tankards, towering row after row', to pistols on the wall and to the lurking dogs. There is similar realism in much of the dialogue, such as Heathcliff's dry remark to Lockwood after the latter has been set upon by the dogs: 'They won't meddle with persons who touch nothing.'

Yet there is much here that goes beyond realism. Heathcliff and Catherine are often more like gods or devils than human beings. Heathcliff is a type of the Byronic hero, dark, brooding, passionate, but he has more human moments, such as when he instinctively saves the infant Hareton. Catherine is elemental as well as human, both an archetypal nature goddess and a woman fatally torn between two lovers. In addition, the novel contains fairytale elements. When old Earnshaw, like the merchant in 'Beauty and the Beast', asks what each child wants as a present, their choices have a fairytale significance – Catherine chooses a whip and Hindley a fiddle. What they get instead, 'born' from under the old man's coat, is a dark sprite – Heathcliff. Moreover, the three episodes by which young Catherine is lured from the enchanted safety of her father's park into the dangerous territory of the wolfish Heathcliff echo fairytales which deal with sexual coming of age (Chapters 18, 21 and 22). Catherine's father tries to protect her, but her disobedience is inevitable.

Characterization

As noted in Chapter 1, the characters of *Wuthering Heights* divide according to the two houses in which they live. Nelly herself spans both, although, being an unromantic conservative by nature, she favours Thrushcross Grange, 'tut-tutting' over the goings-on at the Heights. Heathcliff and Catherine, coming from the wilder house, are of course the central characters.

As a child, Heathcliff is quietly stoical; as a man he is vengefully cruel, and cynical about everything except Catherine. Even with regard to her he is no Romeo, accusing her on her deathbed of 'infernal selfishness' and cursing her after she dies: 'May she wake in torment!' His driving force is his desire to avenge himself, first on Hindley for mistreating him, and then on Edgar Linton for marrying Catherine. Only a man of preternatural hatred could pursue his revenge to such lengths. Isabella Linton, whom he marries in order to abuse her and obtain her brother's property, asks some key questions: 'Is Mr Heathcliff a man? If so, is he mad? And if not, is he a devil?' Perhaps the answer is yes on all three counts: he has human passions and desires, and suffers intensely; his obsession with Catherine amounts to madness; and his cruelty and connivance are devilish. Indeed, on another level he is Lucifer, whose bitterness is that of one who has been cast out of heaven.

Catherine Earnshaw is wild, spirited and wilful. She is a true child of the Heights, yet she falls from grace through a fatal flaw: her choice of Edgar Linton over Heathcliff, of culture and refinement over nature and raw vitality. Her mistaken belief that she can have both kills her. One could blame her own perversity. When Nelly ironically asks her where the objection can be to her marrying Edgar, Catherine replies emphatically: 'In my soul and in my heart, I'm convinced I'm wrong!'

Catherine's daughter, whom we will call Cathy, resembles her mother enough to make her father sigh and Heathcliff snarl. In character she is superficially similar. She is spirited but not fundamentally rebellious. She is also loving and dutiful to her father. She mocks Hareton but eventually repents and teaches him to read, enabling him to decipher his own name – which is also that of his ancestor – over the front of the house. Thus she is helping to restore him to his legitimate position in the established social order.

Symbolism and imagery

Related to the theme of imprisonment (see Chapter 4, 'Major Themes') is the symbolic use of windows, doors (and their keys) and walls. They represent openings into possibility, boundaries between phases of life, between people, and between the material and spiritual worlds. When Edgar learns that Catherine is ill, he orders Nelly to shut the window, as if her soul might escape. A page later Catherine threatens suicide 'by a spring from the window' (Ch. 12).

Heathcliff is able to enter the house, like the devil, by a back door negligently left open. When Edgar confronts him, Catherine locks them all in so that her husband must face Heathcliff unaided. When Edgar struggles for the key, she throws it into 'the hottest part of the fire' (Ch. 11). When Heathcliff leaves, he signifies his contempt for boundaries by striking the lock from the door.

A particularly evocative symbol appears in Chapter 22, when the teenage Cathy finds herself stranded outside the perimeter wall of her father's park. Nelly on the inside tries all her keys to open a door, but is powerless to protect her mistress when Heathcliff rides up, like a fairytale wolf in disguise.

Emily's use of imagery is vivid. Heathcliff and his house are 'devilish', 'diabolical' and 'Satanic'. Fire also features, standing for passion and hellfire. Most frequent, however, are images pointing to the animal nature within human nature. Edgar is a 'lamb' that 'threatens like a bull' (Ch. 11). Catherine calls him 'a sucking leverett'. Isabella fears Heathcliff as she would 'a tiger or a venomous serpent' (Ch. 13). Cathy calls Isabella 'an impertinent little monkey' (Ch. 10), while Heathcliff stares at his unfortunate wife 'as one might do at a strange repulsive animal – a centipede from the Indies, for instance' (Ch. 10).

Shakespeare's influence

Emily's knowledge of Shakespeare is apparent in both the plot and characters of *Wuthering Heights*. Witness the emphasis on revenge, the restoration of the 'rightful' order and the use of animal imagery. Heathcliff and Catherine are like Antony and Cleopatra; old Earnshaw's folly in favouring Heathcliff resembles that of Lear and Gloucester with their children; Shakespeare's Edgar, like Emily's, stands for legitimacy in conflict with embittered illegitimacy; while Catherine in her ravings and loss of self resembles Lear. However, the closest parallel is with *The Tempest*. Hareton resembles Caliban and, like him, has been usurped. When Cathy first visits the Heights, Hareton shows her the local delights, just as Caliban shows them to Miranda on his island. Cathy comes to scorn Hareton, as Miranda scorns Caliban. There is even a scene near the end of the novel when she flies at him for daring to stroke her hair. Hareton is degraded by Heathcliff, who teaches him to curse; he is then taught to read by Cathy. In *The Tempest*, Prospero first teaches Caliban language, then degrades him, whereupon he learns to use his language to curse. Both Hareton and Caliban are finally freed and regain their inheritance.

JANE EYRE

Charlotte's best-known novel, published in 1847, can be enjoyed on a number of levels.

Bildungsroman and allegory

One approach is to see the novel as a **Bildungsroman**. We can at the same time compare it to Bunyan's allegory *Pilgrim's Progress*, to which Charlotte herself alludes. We follow Jane's life story, seeing how she learns from her trials. As an orphaned outsider in the Reed family, she is bullied mercilessly by John Reed. The 'wicked stepmother', Aunt Reed rejects her for not being 'sociable and childlike'.

> **KEYWORD**
>
> *Bildungsroman*: a 'novel of education', especially in the German tradition, following the life story and development of one main protagonist. Fielding's *Tom Jones* is an example.

When 10-year-old Jane dares to defend herself against 'Master John', she is locked in the frightening 'red-room' for her 'wickedness'. Her grievances fill her mind 'like a dark deposit in a turbid well', until in the gloom she imagines she sees a spectral presence and has a kind of fit, from which she takes weeks to recover. This illness leads to her being sent away to Lowood School. In effect, her rebellion has at least freed her from the Reed family, although her behaviour is a long way from the controlled self-assertion which she must eventually learn.

At Lowood the saintly and victimized Helen Burns assures Jane, 'It is far better to endure patiently a smart which nobody feels but yourself' (Ch. 6). Jane, however, refuses to let 'the wicked people ... have it all their own own way'. The school is presided over by the puritanical Brocklehurst, who publicly denounces her as a liar. Yet she endures this, helped by Helen's sympathy. The passage ends in a triumphant tone: Jane has learned a lesson – though not the one intended by Brocklehurst.

At Thornfield, Jane develops a mutual attachment to a man twice her age, the enigmatic Rochester. They come to share an understanding and love based on mutual respect. But the real lesson comes when she experiences a bride's worst nightmare: Rochester is already married – and to a madwoman. Jane, however, passes the moral test: she resists the temptation to become his mistress.

Reaching the moral high ground of Marsh End, and winning the support of St John (pronounced Sinjn) Rivers and his two sisters, Jane faces a new temptation: a life of missionary self-denial with Rivers. Charlotte 'saves' her heroine from this marble sepulchre by a 'cry' of telepathic anguish from Rochester. Bertha is conveniently disposed of, and we assume Jane lives happily ever after with Rochester. She has achieved self-realization through suffering.

A Gothic Romance

On one level *Jane Eyre* is a Gothic Romance. There are seemingly supernatural elements early on, when Jane sees herself in the red-room's mirror as a spirit, 'half fairy, half imp', and soon after thinks she sees her uncle's ghost (Ch. 2). However, Gothic gloom descends with a vengeance when she arrives at Thornfield, whose antique stools bear 'traces of half-effaced embroideries, wrought by fingers that for two generations had been coffin-dust' (Ch. 11). This mood increases at the mystery owner's first appearance. In the gathering dusk, his huge dog makes Jane think of the ghostly Gytrash of folktales. Rochester has the face of a man haunted by his past. He is even more Byronic than Heathcliff.

On one level, *Jane Eyre* and *Villette* are Gothic Romances.

The fact that Thornfield is hiding something dreadful is hinted at when Jane compares it with '**Bluebeard**'s castle'. Rochester's secret, his mad wife, is a fearful figure, although, tellingly, when Jane first hears her 'curious laugh' she finds it thrilling. When, in a foreshadowing of things to come, Bertha sets fire to Rochester's bed, Jane hears 'a demoniac laugh – low, suppressed, and deep', and then an inhuman gurgling and moaning. Bertha is often described as an animal: her 'fearful shriek' is like that of a vulture, a demon and a bird of prey; she snarls like a dog. Jane asks herself:

> **KEY FACT**
>
> Bluebeard: in the folktale, Bluebeard warns his wife never to enter a forbidden room in his castle. Overcome by curiosity, she disobeys him and finds it contains the corpses of his previous wives.

> What crime was this, that lived incarnate in this sequestered mansion, and could neither be expelled nor subdued by the owner? – what mystery, that broke out, now in fire and now in blood, at the deadest hours of night?'
>
> (Ch. 20)

This is wonderfully Gothic! But soon we encounter the Gothic sub-genre which epitomized the Victorians' darkest sexual neuroses. After Bertha's attack on Richard Mason, Rochester is anxious to get rid of him before dawn: 'The sun will soon rise.' The doctor finds teeth marks in Mason's arm, and Mason confirms: 'She sucked the blood: she said she'd drain my heart.' Thornfield has become Castle Dracula!

The once-beautiful Bertha is a 'mulatto' from the West Indies – suggesting to the Victorian mind something exotic but dangerous. Contrary to the Victorian ideal (and unlike Jane and Charlotte herself), Bertha is a big woman, possessed of 'virile force' (Ch. 26). She is full of 'vices', and has a 'pigmy intellect' but 'giant propensities'. It is implied that animal sexuality has made her mad.

A moral quagmire

Charlotte begins the novel on firm moral ground. We sympathize with Jane's feisty – even Byronic – rebellion. However, things begin to get bogged down when Rochester appears. Is he, as we are asked to believe, a good man with a bad past? By modern standards, his racy affair with a Parisian opera-dancer is no crime. By Victorian standards he was generous to rescue her daughter Adèle from the 'slime and mud of Paris'. One could even say that he has fulfilled his duty to Bertha. That said, it is surely more to his benefit than hers that she is held prisoner in secret. We wonder if it was rejection and incarceration that drove her mad.

Whatever the truth of this, Rochester's treatment of his 18-year-old governess is shabby by any standards. He tricks her even on their first meeting, when he pretends, for no clear reason, to know nothing of Thornfield's owner. Then, despite a growing affection for her, he proceeds with the charade of his proposed marriage to the shallow Blanche Ingram. He conceals his secret from Jane, despite his debt to her and the threat to her life represented by Bertha. Towards the end of Chapter 20, he poses a hypothetical case of a man who hopes to start afresh by 'overleaping an obstacle of custom' (committing bigamy!). When she primly advises him to seek a higher wisdom than her own, he almost comes clean – then reverts to sarcastic praise of Blanche.

Rochester's bizarre impersonation of an old female gypsy is another example of gratuitous trickery (Ch. 19). Even his proposal to Jane (Ch. 23) springs out of the trick he has played on Blanche to test her love. After the abortive wedding, he even tries moral blackmail: 'You fling me back on lust for a passion – vice for an occupation?' (Ch. 27).

As for Jane, she has been wilfully blind to the warning signs, and overly keen to excuse Rochester – until the would-be bigamy is revealed and she takes the morally conventional course. Thus spurning illicit passion, she is cast on the cold Christian charity of the passionless St John Rivers. She is half-tempted to give in to his conviction that it is her Christian duty to marry him. In their different ways, respectively icy and volcanic, Rivers and Rochester are equally domineering. Jane is attracted to this, as perhaps was Charlotte. In the end, she has asserted her need for independence and passionate love, but what are we to make of the fact that she is now content to serve the blind, one-handed Rochester?

Superb style

One of Charlotte's strengths is her use of symbolism, as in the veil-rending incident. Then there is the proposal scene in the garden, with the lightning-split chestnut tree (see Chapter 2, 'How to Approach the Brontës' Work'). At the start of the book the pictures viewed by the young Jane in Bewick symbolize her present and future life, especially those evoking coldness and desolation. As in Charlotte's other novels, too, the moon is both a cue for heightened awareness and a symbol of natural wisdom. Charlotte's imagery is similarly enriching. Jane's paintings are evocatively described (Ch. 13): the shipwreck in the first foreshadows things to come, while the second depicts 'the great mother'. The third, depicting an iceberg, exemplifies the images of coldness and desolation that throughout the novel Charlotte opposes to those of heat and passion. Rivers is associated with cold marble, Rochester with fire, the sun and volcanoes.

Charlotte's scene-setting spell-bindingly creates atmosphere, as when she first meets Rochester and in the proposal scene. Her variation of pace is also excellent. For example, the jumbled confusion of the night when Bertha attacks her brother gives way to the intimate tranquillity of the garden at dawn, and Rochester's near-confession. Notice, too, the innovative use of the present tense at moments of dramatic tension, as in Chapter 23, and when Jane tends Mason in Chapter 20. In Chapter 17 it is coupled with another of Charlotte's techniques, the use of questions:

And where is Mr Rochester?

He comes in last: I am not looking at the arch, yet I see him enter. I try to concentrate my attention …

SHIRLEY

Charlotte's second novel, *Shirley* (1850) ambitiously portrays the social problems caused by trade restrictions during the Napoleonic wars. The author quickly declares her earthy intention: to offer 'something as unromantic as Monday morning, when all who have work wake with the consciousness that they must rise and betake themselves thereto' (Ch. 1). The irony is probably intentional: a major theme is the hardship caused by unemployment when mill-owners brought in machinery – leading to the Luddite riots, in which looms were smashed and mills burned down.

Social comment

Shirley is meticulously researched, which adds interest but occasionally weighs down the narrative. It also uses settings which Charlotte knew well, which shows in some very fine descriptions. Charlotte presents unemployment and desperate poverty with sympathy and some understanding, but she is too much of a Tory not to present the protesters as a misguided rabble led astray by bad men. Their leaders, such as Barraclough and Moses (Ch. 8) are self-serving and pretentiously stupid. Others are 'strangers – emissaries from the large towns [and] not members of the operative class' (Ch. 22).

Only when she deals with individuals does Charlotte's true humanity emerge. Her portrayal of the redundant mill-hand William Farren is touching. His homely assessment of the situation and his honest pride remind us of similar characters in Dickens's *Hard Times*, Mrs Gaskell's *North and South* (both published after *Shirley*), and the soldier Williams in *Henry V*: 'It's out o' no ill-will that I'm here, for my part; it's just to make a effort to get things straightened, for they're sorely a-crooked' (*Shirley*, Ch. 8).

A novel of ideas

Farren later echoes a sentiment expressed by Charlotte as narrator. In his words, 'Human natur', taking it i' the' lump, is nought by selfishness.' This, indeed, is one of a number of ideas explored –

sometimes in rather unconvincing dialogue. Gerard Moore, as a mill-owner fighting bankruptcy, is essentially selfish. He opposes war purely because it damages trade. (Charlotte herself was a patriot and admired Wellington.) Charlotte makes it clear that he goes too far when he tries to clear his debts by marrying Shirley.

A role for women

Another idea explored is that of a role for women. Caroline sickens and almost pines away for lack of purpose: 'What was I created for, I wonder? Where is my place in the world? ... Ah! I see ... that is the question which most old maids are puzzled to solve' (Ch. 10). When she asks her uncle if she can become a governess, he dismisses her request as ridiculous. The chapter in which she subsequently visits two 'old maids' shows Charlotte at her most sensitive and humane.

Shirley herself suffers none of Caroline's agonies of purpose. Rich, beautiful, self-confident – and rather unbelievable as a character – she enjoys running her estate, organizing rambles with Caroline and distributing largesse. Peter Davies has commented that she resembles Jane Austen's Emma, equally patronizing, but not subjected to the same authorial scrutiny (*The Brontës*, 2000). Charlotte said that the character of Shirley represented what Emily might have been in happier circumstances. Certainly Shirley's physical robustness, for example when she leads Caroline through the woods in an attempt to warn Moore of an attack on his mill, resembles Emily's. The incident when Shirley cauterizes her own wound after being bitten by a dog is based directly on Emily, who did the same thing herself.

Shirley is almost a sort of honorary man, jocularly calling herself 'Captain Keeldar' and speaking in military terms to the soldierly Rector Helstone. She evicts the boorish Donne for lampooning Yorkshiremen, declaring later: 'Had I been a gentleman, I believe I should have helped him off the premises by dint of physical force' (Ch. 16). She stands up to the sexist Joe Scott, and even takes on Milton, claiming that his Eve is merely an image of his cook! She goes on to make a pagan-feminist speech on the primacy of woman and Mother Nature (Ch. 18). Caroline, by way of contrast, is more concerned with the lack of a human mother, and it is surely wish-fulfilment on Charlotte's part when she is reunited with the mother she thought was dead.

Shirley's assertiveness does not prevent her from revealing Charlotte's usual adulation of the male ego: 'He is a noble being. I tell you when they are good, they are the lords of creation – they are the sons of God … Indisputably, a great, good, handsome man is the first of created things' (Ch. 12). Neither does it stop her handing over the management of her estate with a grateful sigh as soon as she has a husband to manage it for her.

Wit and pace

Except when Caroline is moping, the tone is much lighter than in Charlotte's other novels. The conversations between the two heroines are often fanciful – and delightfully unrealistic – as when they fantasize about a herd of whales and Shirley declares she would hate to be capsized by 'the patriarch bull' (Ch. 13). However, there is fine satirical wit in Charlotte's portrayal of the curates. The novel also has scenes of well-paced and exciting action, such as the mob attack on the mill in Chapter 19, an account echoed in Gaskell's *North and South*.

VILLETTE

Charlotte's last novel, *Villette* (1853) is her most controversial and most autobiographical. Revisiting her painful experience of Brussels and her unrequited love for Heger, it reworks in more depth the material set out in her first novel, *The Professor*. It tells the story of Lucy Snowe, a retiring young woman for whom a teaching job abroad leads to love and self-discovery.

Charlotte or Lucy Snowe?

As narrator, Lucy Snowe provides an ample commentary on events and her own state of mind. It is often difficult to distinguish between her and Charlotte, especially when prejudices are aired. We become aware of the paradoxes in Lucy, and probably in Charlotte herself. Like William Crimsworth in *The Professor*, she bravely sets out with little money in hand and no job to go to. At the same time, the language conveys her fears. Her budding hopes are 'kept in check by the secret but ceaseless consciousness of anxiety lying in wait on enjoyment, like a tiger crouched in a jungle' (Ch. 7).

Lucy Snowe's description of all things Continental, and especially Belgian, borders on a xenophobia which may simply voice Charlotte's prejudices, as in *The Professor* and *Jane Eyre*. The port at which she lands is Boue-Marine (Ocean Mud). Even the name 'Villette' (Little town) is disparaging. Lucy's pupils are a 'swinish multitude' who cannot cope with intellectual effort (Ch. 9). Here and in *The Professor*, the girls are described as stupid, shallow, vain – and even fat and big-eared! The novel is also marred by anti-Catholicism. Hence in the school, 'Each mind was being reared in slavery' (Ch. 14).

Not Jane Eyre

Yet Lucy Snowe is complex and fascinating. She is less assertive and more solitary than Jane Eyre, and more resigned. Thus she adapts to a stultifying life with the invalid Miss Marchmont. She fits into the pinched world of Madame Beck's school, rarely venturing outside and calmly tolerates her spying. She often chooses solitude and makes no real friends. She is 'a mere looker-on at life' (Ch. 14). Above all, she represses her feelings and assumes that she is too plain for any man to notice her. She is like the ghostly nun, supposedly buried alive centuries before, whom she encounters in the garden and attic. At key moments feelings begin to break through, and her icy calm begins to thaw, but she schools herself to self-denial: 'About the present, it was better to be stoical; about the future – such a future as mine – to be dead' (Ch. 12).

Lucy becomes more like Jane Eyre as she begins to long 'for something to fetch me out of my present existence, and lead me upwards and onwards' (Ch. 12) and when she finds herself thrust into challenging situations – as when she faces her first class and deals with a troublemaker by locking her in the cupboard! She meets another challenge when the impatient and demanding Paul Emmanuel makes her take on a part in the school play at short notice. After being locked in the attic to learn her part, she rises to the occasion, significantly applying her own interpretation to the unappealing role.

Lucy's path to wholeness, however, is uneven. Her nervous breakdown has long been waiting in the wings. As so often in this novel, the weather is made to reflect the mood. Her 'peculiarly agonizing depression' and physical illness are attended by 'equinoctial storms' and 'sounding hurricane'. In her fever, Lucy realizes for the first time, that the school is 'crushing as the slab of a tomb', escapes and pays her visit to a Catholic priest, then collapses completely.

She is saved by a brief return to something like family life, with the Brettons, who feed her nourishing seed-cake – as Miss Temple does the Lowood girls in *Jane Eyre*. But it is ultimately Lucy's growing relationship with Paul Emmanuel, the first man to have really noticed her, that ensures her recovery.

Female roles

Villette can be seen as a psychodrama, its characters, especially the female ones, representing aspects of Lucy Snowe, or at least role models. As a narrator, she is elusive. We never know anything about her parents, and the catastrophe which leads to her becoming Miss Marchmont's nurse-companion is described only as an extended metaphor relating to a shipwreck (Ch. 4), reminiscent of *Jane Eyre*.

Miss Marchmont, who asks, 'For what crime was I condemned, after twelve months of bliss, to undergo thirty years of sorrow?', reminds us of Dickens's Miss Havisham. She represents a role model for Lucy – and, ironically, one which at the end of the novel Lucy could actually become. The manipulative Madame Beck, controlling her little empire by espionage, is another. Lucy is identified with her when we see her spying on Madame Beck while Madame Beck spies on her. Lucy feels mingled scorn and affection for little Polly, who becomes Paulina. Yet Paulina represents what Lucy might have been had she been blessed with looks and money.

The buried nun is certainly an aspect of Lucy, but the most outlandish representation of womanhood is Madame Walravens, the bitter old lady responsible for blighting Paul Emmauel's youthful prospects. The novel's Gothic flavour intensifies when this deformed, wizened and hag-like personage appears. Sent to her with a basket of fruit by Madame Beck, Lucy resembles Little Red Riding Hood, or another fairytale figure sent with gifts to appease a witch. Described as 'the sorceress' and 'the evil fairy', Madame Walravens embodies the Goddess in her dark winter form. Her name suggests incarceration and death. Moreover, she emerges from a painting of a nun, symbolically warning what a repressed and unfulfilled woman may become.

A warning of a different kind is sounded by the great actress Vashti, whom Lucy sees perform. Her name is that of a biblical queen who refused to show off her beauty for the gratification of kings. A woman who plays many parts, Vashti seems to be killing herself by the effort. She is a model of the woman artist, both praised and rejected by bourgeois society. Tellingly, her performance sets the theatre ablaze – literally! She is thus a natural sister of mad Bertha in *Jane Eyre*, a vessel for pyromaniacal female rage.

A happy ending?

Lucy's hero is sent off to the West Indies on a kind of fairytale quest from which he will probably never return. The ending is superficially ambiguous, anticipating modern novels with alternative endings, such as John Fowles's *The French Lieutenant's Woman*. Perhaps this springs from Charlotte being caught between her own pessimism and her public's expectations – or perhaps she is just toying with us ironically. At any rate, Lucy speaks of the wait for her lover's return as 'the three happiest years of my life', suggesting that either his return was an anticlimax or else he was lost at sea. All the signs suggest the latter: the note of pathetically doomed hope in the repeated 'he is coming'; the dreadful omen of the wind's banshee wail; the 'destroying angel of tempest'. She hints that if we imagine a happy ending, then we are naively deluded.

The ending of *Villette* is ambiguous.

Style

In *Villette*, Charlotte returns to the immediacy of first-person narrative. This compels our attention and sympathy, but the technique sometimes gives way to excessive commentary. In addition, we may find it irritating that occasionally the text reads as if Charlotte herself is addressing us in what should be a marginal note: 'Reader, if in the course of this work, you find that my opinion of Dr John undergoes modification, excuse this inconsistency' (Ch. 18).

Another stylistic feature that works with uneven success is the use of metaphor and especially **personification**. In Chapter 4, an extended maritime metaphor for the 'shipwreck' of Lucy's life foreshadows the ending of the novel. But Charlotte's use of personification can be excessive, as in Chapter 21, when Lucy conducts a long conversation with Reason about her romantic hopes. A further use of personification appears in the allusions to Bunyan's *Pilgrim's Progress*.

KEYWORD

Personification: a kind of metaphor in which something is described as if it were a person.

Charlotte's effective use of weather to create atmosphere is equalled by her use of settings, such as the school garden (reminiscent of Thornfield's garden in *Jane Eyre*). At times this is combined atmospherically with Charlotte's trademark use of the present tense, as in Miss Marchmont's beautiful evocation of her doomed romance (Ch. 4).

THE TENANT OF WILDFELL HALL

Wildfell Hall was published in 1848. In the preface to the second edition, Anne Brontë warns us that the novel pulls no punches: it will not be 'ladylike'. Hence, although Anne was ostensibly the most conventional Christian of the sisters, and had a passionate moral purpose in writing the novel, she offended many contemporary readers by her portrayal of debauchery, infidelity and violence. Modern readers may be deterred by the very fact that is has a moral purpose. However, in many ways it equals the novels discussed above. It lacks the raw passion of *Wuthering Heights* and the sheer poetry of *Jane Eyre*, but it is livelier than *Villette* and its characters are, arguably, more acutely observed than those of any other Brontë novel. Above all, its vigorous plot makes it a real page-turner!

Narrative structure

Anne's narrative technique is original and well handled, although owing something to *Wuthering Heights* and *Jane Eyre*. Like Emily's novel, much of the story is told in flashback by a female narrator framed by a male one. It also features a runaway wife, men behaving badly, violence and an alternation of settings which feature different types of behaviour and atmosphere. As in *Jane Eyre*, a disastrous marriage initially prevents a happier one, a woman flees from a man and conceals her identity, there is a fortunate legacy and the death of a bad spouse makes way for a good one.

Anne had to make Helen almost saintly.

However, there are important differences. Unlike Lockwood in *Wuthering Heights*, Gilbert Markham is a major participant in the story, not just its vehicle. Moreover, we are 15 chapters into the novel before we look over his shoulder to read Helen Graham's diary. When we do, we are obliged to reassess Helen and, indeed, the whole situation. In fact, we realize that Gilbert is the ultimate in unreliable narrators, since he has so badly misread the signs as to assault Helen's brother, mistaking him for a rival suitor. One consequence of this structure is that we realize that what we took to be the start of the story is actually the middle. When the diary ends, the past begins to overtake the present. When Helen goes to tend her sick husband, we again share Gilbert's lack of information, until he begins to read her letters to her brother.

Settings are important structuring features in the story. Gilbert's home at Linden-car is pleasantly cosy. Here he is in the bosom of his family. When the novel begins, he looks set to marry the essentially ordinary Eliza and follow in his father's conservative farming footsteps, but the beautiful stranger's arrival upsets this applecart. When he leaves his gentle lowland farm and climbs the steep slope to the wilds of Wildfell Hall, he is risking safety and comfort for a higher goal. When the novel shifts to Grassdale Manor to depict the decline of Helen's marriage, an altogether darker and more turbulent world appears.

Another original feature of the novel is that until Helen thrusts her diary into Gilbert's hand, we may well expect it to proceed smoothly towards marriage, like so many nineteenth-century novels. But in reassessing the situation, we realize that this story has actually begun with a marriage, and we cannot countenance a new one until the old has been exorcized. Added to this, whereas Rochester is the man of experience who will initiate Jane, the experienced one in this novel is Helen, not Gilbert.

Characters

Some feminist critics suggest that Gilbert is an oppressor, like Huntingdon. Although Gilbert is portrayed as having faults, whereas Helen's main one is excessive virtue, it at least seems unlikely that Anne Brontë intended this interpretation. Whatever her moral purposes, she sets out to achieve them by presenting realistic characters.

Presented as a saviour, a good shepherd tending his lambs (see Ch. 19), Gilbert resembles another good shepherd obliged to wait for the death of a bad husband – Hardy's Gabriel Oak. But Gilbert is more realistically portrayed than stout-hearted Gabriel. His imperfections are manifest. Already interested in Helen, he still flirts with Eliza. (Interestingly, Anne is not at all disapproving.) His fierce denial of local gossip turns to bitterness when he misconstrues Lawrence's visit, and he violently assaults the innocent man (Ch. 15). In the next chapter he is unkind to Helen's son, and cold to her: 'I felt glad to have it in my power to torment her.' In short, he is human.

Huntingdon is a brilliant creation, a convincing counterblast to the romanticized concept of the Byronic hero. Through him, Anne demonstrates that although his type may seem exciting – rich, suave, wicked and wild – life with such a man is likely to be hell. The beautiful but shallow Rosalie Murray, in *Agnes Grey*, marries a man who is similar in some ways, and soon regrets it. Yet even Huntingdon is no caricature: he is weak rather than evil. We see him discomfited in the library (Ch. 19) when, for all his smooth talk, he cannot charm Helen's aunt. We see his vanity: 'drinking spoils one's good looks' (Ch. 22). His ill treatment of his favourite dog (Ch. 24) stems from petulant ill humour rather than real cruelty. After flirting openly with Annabella, he quotes Shakespeare in his own defence, and makes a plausible effort to placate his wife, though in the same breath warning her not to drive him away by 'too much severity'. A complete egotist, he sees his son first as a rival for his wife's attention, and later as an opportunity to create a copy of his own vices.

As for Helen, Anne had to make her near perfect in order for the public to excuse her leaving her husband. She is genuinely pious and sincerely hopes to convert her dissolute husband. Her care of him in his self-induced decline is almost saintly, especially if one considers that restoring him to health will restore her to servitude. At the end she tries to save him, telling him: 'God is Infinite Wisdom, and Power, and Goodness – and *Love*.' When it seems he cannot repent, she consoles herself with 'the blessed confidence that, through whatever, purging fires the erring spirit may be doomed to pass – whatever fate awaits it, still, it is not lost, and God, who hateth nothing that He hath made, *will* bless it in the end!' Nevertheless, she can be over-austere, and even rude at times, unsympathetic to the foibles of others (she hates small talk). When she does smile, it is as if the sun has come out from behind a dark cloud.

Lesser characters are all portrayed with real insight: the unctuous and dissembling Hargrave, who momentarily tempts Helen; the dissolutely depressive Lowborough, made to swallow the bitter pill of his wife's infidelity with Huntingdon; blundering Hattersley, who begins as a drunken brute but has just enough sense to take Helen's advice and reform himself; the shameless Annabella; the reserved Mr Lawrence; and Helen's supportive 'sisters' Millicent and Esther. Even quite minor characters spring to life delightfully in Anne's deft and often ironic profiles:

> Mrs Wilson was more brilliant than ever, with her budgets of fresh news and old scandal, strung together with trivial questions and remarks, and oft repeated observations, uttered apparently for the sole purpose of denying a moment's rest to her inexhaustible organs of speech.
>
> (Ch. 4)

Perfectly paced drama

Anne's astute characterization is complemented by a telling use of dialogue and superb stage management. We see the consequence of Huntingdon's pettish, nervy inebriation:

> 'Be quick, Benson – do have done with that infernal clatter!' cried his master – 'And *don't* bring the cheese! – unless you want to make me sick outright.'
>
> Benson, in some surprise, removed the cheese, and did his best to effect a quiet and speedy clearance of the rest, but, unfortunately, there was a rumple in the carpet, caused by the hasty pushing back of his master's chair …
>
> (Ch. 30)

Another superb scene occurs when Huntingdon's friends are staying at Grassdale (Ch. 31). We move from the grim humour of the drunken Grimsby mistakenly pouring his tea into the sugar bowl, to the ugly scene when Lowborough burns Hattersley's hand, and the latter abuses his own sobbing wife, strikes Hargrave for defending his sister and then hurls a footstool at the much amused Huntingdon. This equals some of the violent scenes in *Wuthering Heights*, but is presented not as cosmic drama but as tawdry degradation.

Symbolism and imagery

Much of Anne's scene-setting is very fine. Take, for example, Wildfell Hall itself, gaunt and neglected (like its occupant), and with its topiary bushes grown into fantastic and rather Gothic shapes. More frequently, there are moments of fresh and natural description as in a view of the sea, 'deep violet blue – not deadly calm, but covered with glinting breakers – diminutive white specks twinkling on its bosom, and scarcely to be distinguished by the keenest vision, from the little-sea mews that sported above' (Ch. 7).

When Anne uses symbolism and imagery, both are fairly explicit. For example, Helen's painting of two doves (Ch. 18) clearly indicates her ideal love, though the dark group of Scotch firs may foreshadow her difficult marriage. Later, Helen tries to persuade Gilbert that 'to regret the exchange of earthly pleasures for the joys of Heaven, is as if the grovelling caterpillar should lament that it must one day quit the nibbled leaf to soar aloft and flutter through the air' (Ch. 45). More poignantly, she makes him a gift of a winter rose, which symbolizes herself: 'This rose is not so fragrant as a summer flower, but it has stood through hardship none of *them* could bear.'

THE POEMS

Opinions differ widely on the quality of the sisters' poems, though most people agree that Emily's are the best. Many of the poems spring out of the passionate childhood worlds of Angria and Gondal.

All three sisters wrote poems about liberty, solitude, love and paradise. They all fell too readily into conventional rhyming and metre – even Emily at times – and none of them is noted for originality of diction or ideas. They all refer often to death, loss, gloom and imprisonment, and liberally use the words 'drear', 'dreary', 'anguish', 'desolation' and 'despair' – lightened here and there by 'joy' and 'liberty'. Where they succeed, they do so largely through word music coupled with sincerity of feeling.

Charlotte

Charlotte's poems are interesting in relation to her novels. 'Master and Pupil', for example, hints at her relationship with Heger, and at the fictional relationships between her heroines and their men, especially between Lucy Snowe and Paul Emmanuel: 'If I but faltered in the way,/ His anger fiercely flamed.' When the master calls 'Jane!' from the window, and she joyfully responds, we think of Jane Eyre. But when the pupil's success only opens 'a secret, inward wound', with the threat of shipwreck, we find ourselves in the final chapter of *Villette*.

'Reason' reveals another recurring theme: passion compels Charlotte to seek love, while reason tells her that she is condemned to loneliness: 'Unloved I love, unwept, I weep,/ Grief I restrain, hope I repress.'

Anne

Charlotte described Anne's poems as 'sweet' and they do have a lucid simplicity that reminds us of Wordsworth, especially when coupled with longing for a 'paradise lost', as in 'A Voice from the Dungeon'. Some are really hymns or prayers, and many are inspired by Christian faith. Like Emily, Anne speaks of dungeons and liberty, but to her, liberty is salvation. However, her Gondal poems are more rugged. The 'song' beginning 'We know where deepest lies the snow' is a fine example, in which a recently hunted Republican, now turned hunter, voices Anne's compassion in his distaste for persecution.

'A Word to the Elect' is a heartfelt but well-argued reply to the Calvinist doctrine of the 'Chosen Few', rejected by Helen in *Wildfell Hall*. 'Farewell to Thee, but not Farewell' is a wonderfully positive elegy to Emily, while the brave-hearted 'Last Lines', written when Anne learned that her own illness was terminal, is powerfully affecting.

Emily

Emily's poems are usually about escape from the world, either into union with nature or into the world of spirit: 'I'm happiest when most away/ I can bear my soul from its home of clay'. She longs to be 'only spirit wandering wide/ Through infinite immensity'. Many of her poems contemplate death, often seen as a return to nature, as in 'In the earth, the earth, thou shalt be laid', which uses a dialogue form to give alternate views of death. As so often with Emily, the choice of words is not remarkable, but the arrangement of them is. Repetition is used liturgically, as in many of Emily's best poems, for example 'A.G.A.' (Augusta Geraldine Almeda, the Byronic Gondal heroine), in which each verse begins with 'Sleep brings' and a masterful combination of dactylic rhythm and spondaic stanza endings, anticipating Thomas Hardy's poem 'In Tenebris', gives a keen sense of desolation:

> Sleep brings no strength to me,
> No power renewed to brave,
> I only sail a wilder sea,
> A darker wave.

Many of Emily's poems are passionate, pagan and individualistic, as in 'No Coward Soul is Mine', in which she casually dismisses the 'thousand creeds/ That move men's hearts' in favour of her own anchorage on 'The steadfast rock of Immortality'. Some describe mystical experience: 'Mute music soothes my breast – unuttered harmony'. Others are deeply mysterious and atmospheric, as in the stylistically innovative 'I'll Come when Thou art Saddest', which uses an unusual rhyme scheme and alliteration to sweep the reader into a world of 'strange sensations' heralding 'a sterner power'.

Emily's most famous poem, however, is 'Remembrance' (which also has a Gondal name, 'R. Alcona to J. Brenzaida'). The poem's relentless rhythm, repetition, understated nature imagery and oxymorons ('rapturous pain … divinest anguish') convey a powerful sense of bereavement and lost love.

***

❋ ❋ ❋ *SUMMARY* ❋ ❋ ❋

● *Wuthering Heights* is a 'framed' narrative, with a mythical dimension and fairytale elements. Its characters fall into two groups. It is influenced by Shakespeare.

● *Jane Eyre* is both a life story and a Gothic romance. Its heroine seeks self-realization.

● *Shirley* is a novel of social concerns, written in the third person, with two heroines.

● *Villette* is the story of Lucy Snowe's journey to wholeness, told by herself.

● *Wildfell Hall* sets out to show what happens when a woman marries a bad man.

● Of the sisters' poems, Emily's are the most original.

6 Contemporary Critical Approaches

Charlotte was the sister who achieved the greatest acclaim in her own lifetime. Anne attracted less critical attention, although *Wildfell Hall* sold well. As for *Wuthering Heights*, most reviewers were either baffled or horrified. A feature of the early critical reception was the speculation over the identities of Currer, Acton and Ellis Bell. Counter to the sisters' intentions, their pseudonyms led to a preoccupation with their gender and identity. This was exaggerated by the apparently autobiographical nature of *Jane Eyre*. To Charlotte's acute embarrassment, her dedication of the latter's second edition to Thackeray led to the rumour that 'Currer Bell' was Thackeray's governess, since his own wife, like Rochester's, was mentally ill and institutionalized.

THE POEMS

It was the favourable reception of the sisters' poems that encouraged them to pursue the publication of their novels – despite sales being limited to two copies! The poets were praised for 'good, wholesome, refreshing, vigorous poetry'. One discerning reader notes that the family's 'instinct for song' was shared 'in very unequal proportions; requiring in the case of Acton Bell [Anne], the indulgences of affection … and rising in that of Ellis [Emily], into an inspiration' (*Athenaeum*, 4 July 1846). *The Spectator*, commenting after the publication of *Jane Eyre*, was more critical, accusing the 'Bells' of disregarding 'the nature of poetical composition'.

CHARLOTTE'S NOVELS

It is easy to understand how *Wuthering Heights* and *The Tenant of Wildfell Hall* might have shocked Victorian moralists, but it harder to understand why some critics called Charlotte's novels 'coarse'. However, even they usually acknowledged that her talent was original and refreshing.

Jane Eyre

Charlotte's first published novel was on the whole well received, although it was criticized for the same features for which it was appreciated. What to some critics was individualism was to others arrogance or perversity; what some praised as realistic and passionate others called coarse and improper.

The plot was called both interesting and improbable:

> It is a story of surpassing interest, riveting the attention from the very first chapter, and sustaining it by a copiousness of incident rare indeed in our modern school of novelists … the incidents … are, if anything, too much crowded.
>
> *(The Critic, 30 October 1847)*

> The story is not only of singular interest, naturally evolved, unflagging to the last, but it fastens itself upon your attention, and will not leave you … There are some defects … There is, indeed, too much melodrama and improbability.
>
> (G.H. Lewes, *Fraser's Magazine*, December 1847)

> The plot is most extravagantly improbable.
>
> *(Christian Remembrancer, April 1848)*

Most reviewers commented on the characterization. H.F. Chorley admires the way in which Rochester and Jane 'travel over each other's minds till, in a puzzled and uncomfortable manner enough, they come to a mutual understanding' (*Athenaeum*, 23 October 1847). G.H. Lewes perceptively mixes praise for Charlotte's realism with reservations about her ability to portray male characters. In a similar vein, the reader for the *Christian Remembrancer* notes that 'Mr Rochester … is as clearly the vision of a woman's fancy, as the heroine is the image of a woman's heart', also noting his 'Byronic gloom and appetising mystery' (*Christian Remembrancer*, April 1848).

One negative review came from *The Spectator*, wary of offending its family readership: 'There is a low tone of behaviour (rather than of morality) in the book; and, what is worse than all, neither the heroine nor hero attracts sympathy.'

The *Christian Remembrancer* is unhappy about Charlotte's ire: 'Never was there a better hater. Every page burns with moral Jacobinism.' This same reviewer calls Charlotte's attempt to satirize the upper classes in Blanche Ingram and her mother 'a most decided failure' owing to plebeian ignorance. Elizabeth Rigby echoes this view, and represents the 'morally outraged' end of the critical spectrum. She accuses Charlotte of 'making an unworthy character [Rochester] interesting in the eyes of the reader'. As for Jane herself, 'almost every word she utters offends us ... in either her pedantry, stupidity, or gross vulgarity'. Although admiring Charlotte's style and intellect, Rigby condemns the individualism praised by other commentators, regarding it as anti-Christian (*Quarterly Review*, December 1848).

Shirley and *Villette*

After *Jane Eyre*, *Shirley* was widely considered a disappointment. This may be in part because Charlotte had to research the subject, rather than the idea springing naturally from personal experience. Added to this, she had abandoned the immediacy of first-person narrative. Both plot and characters were thought unengaging and artificial. Even G.H. Lewes, comparing *Shirley* with *Jane Eyre*, found the former unrealistic, coarser, lacking in passion and its characters 'almost all disagreeable' (*Edinburgh Review*, January 1850). The *Daily News* (October 1849) echoed the common gender-based praise and criticism of Charlotte: '*Shirley* is the anatomy of the female heart ... The merit of the work lies in the variety, beauty and truth of its female character. Not one of its men are genuine.'

Neither *Shirley* nor *Villette* was much accused of coarseness, although the flippant portrayal of the curates in *Shirley* – ironically one of the things that Charlotte *did* know from personal experience – was called disrespectful. In other respects, *Villette* was judged to fall somewhere between *Jane Eyre* and *Shirley*. George Eliot called it 'a still more wonderful book than *Jane Eyre* ... almost preternatural in its power (letter to Mrs Charles Bray, 15 February 1853). At the other end of the scale, Matthew Arnold, who had met Charlotte, gets personal: 'Hideous, undelightful, convulsed, constricted ... one of the most utterly disagreeable books I have ever read – and having seen her makes it more so' (Letter to A.H. Clough, 1853). Elsewhere he writes: 'the writer's mind contains nothing but hunger, rebellion and rage, and therefore that is all that she can, in fact, put into her book' (Letter to Mrs Forster, 14 April 1853). Though extreme, he has a point – and one which Virginia Woolf later took up (see next chapter). Charlotte does express an unresolved, angry yearning, though modern readers may not blame her for it.

Harriet Martineau's related criticism is that the book is 'almost intolerably painful', much of this pain stemming from the female characters' preoccupation with love, and 'the writer's tendency to describe the need of being loved' (*Daily News*, 3 Feb. 1853). This touched a raw nerve for Charlotte: she broke off her friendship with Martineau. *The Spectator*, too, speaks of the book's morbidity, the over-indulgence of Lucy Snowe's 'spasms of heart-agony' and of the writer's 'hunger of the heart'.

On the level of plot, some critics were disappointed. Charlotte had returned to what she knew, but the result was a 'defective' plot that lacked 'incident' (*Eclectic Review*, March 1853). *The Spectator* (12 February 1853) spoke for many: 'Of plot, strictly taken as a series of coherent events all leading to a common result, there is none.' To at least one discerning reviewer, however, *Villette* is evidence that 'The democratic principle has ordered romance to descend from the thrones and evacuate the palace' (*Putnam's Monthly Magazine*, May 1853). This reviewer praises the novel's portrayal of ordinary people in mundane circumstances – which anticipates novelists such as Proust, Joyce and Woolf.

Readers were generally positive about the realistic characterization. Many were struck by Paul Emmanuel. *The Spectator* (12 February

1853) called him 'one of the oddest but most real mixtures of the good and disagreeable, of the generous and the little, that a hunter after oddities could wish for his cabinet of curiosities'. Some thought him too ridiculous to be the heroine's choice, but then some thought that the heroine herself was too perverse. One reviewer perceptively praises the way in which he is gradually revealed: 'The skill of the treatment is shown in the gradual melting of the dislike of Paul, until it is entirely replaced by esteem' (*Putnam's Monthly Magazine*, May 1853).

Some reviewers, such as Harriet Martineau and Anne Mozley, commented on the book's anti-Catholic prejudice. Others focused on the style, many agreeing that it had 'clearness and power' resulting from mastery over its subject matter but that it was marred by an overambitious attempt 'to paint by highly figurative language the violent emotions of the heart ... sometimes done at such length, and with so much obscurity from straining after figure and allusion, as to become tedious' (*The Spectator*, 12 February 1853) (see Chapter 5, 'Major Works').

WUTHERING HEIGHTS

In Emily's own lifetime and for decades after it, *Wuthering Heights* received some bewildered praise but no in-depth analysis. The words 'strange', 'powerful', 'repulsive' and 'improbable' were often used to describe it. Sidney Dobell was one of the few who detected 'the stamp of high genius': 'It is the unformed writing of a giant's hand: the "large utterance" of a baby god' (*Palladium*, September 1850).

Even this speaks of the novel as 'unformed'; less impressed readers described it as something rough-hewn and in need of refinement: 'This is a strange book. It is not without evidences of considerable power: but, as a whole, it is wild, confused, disjointed and improbable.' While admiring its ruggedness, the reviewer reminds the author of the artist's duty to 'modify and in some cases refine what he beholds in the ordinary world' (*Examiner*, 8 January 1848). Charlotte encouraged this view in her preface to a posthumous edition: '*Wuthering Heights* was hewn in a wild workshop, with simple tools, out of homely materials.' She even comments that she scarcely thinks it 'right or advisable to create things like Heathcliff'.

Many readers were simply overwhelmed:

> In *Wuthering Heights* the reader is shocked, disgusted, almost sickened by details of cruelty, inhumanity, and the most diabolical hate and vengeance, and anon comes passages of powerful testimony to the supreme power of love – even over demons in the human form.
>
> (*Douglas Jerrold's Weekly Newspaper*, 15 January 1848)

More picturesquely:

> There is an old saying that those who eat toasted cheese at night will dream of Lucifer. The author of W*uthering Heights* has evidently eaten toasted cheese. How a human being could have attempted such a book as the present without committing suicide before he had finished a dozen chapters, is a mystery. It is a compound of vulgar depravity and unnatural horrors, such as we might suppose a person, inspired by a mixture of brandy and gunpowder, might write for the edification of fifth-rate blackguards.
>
> (*Graham's Magazine*, July 1848)

ANNE'S NOVELS

Agnes Grey attracted little critical attention; it seemed insipid beside *Wuthering Heights*, with which it was published. *Wildfell Hall* received more notice, but mostly in a negative light. Accusations of coarseness were uppermost. Despite Anne's moral purpose, critics and ordinary readers complained that the novel revelled in debauchery. One wonders why so many people bought the book! Charlotte hardly helped Anne's cause by saying in a biographical notice in 1850 that she could not wonder at the novel's unfavourable reception because: 'The choice of subject was an entire mistake.'

One reviewer accused the author of having 'a morbid love of the coarse, not to say of the brutal' (*The Spectator*, 8 July 1848). Another

Many Victorian readers were shocked by the Brontës.

warned against the book's 'profane expressions, inconceivably coarse language, and revolting scenes and descriptions' (*Sharpe's London Magazine*). Again, it was 'one of the coarsest books which we ever perused [with a] perpetual tendency to relapse into that class of ideas, expressions, and circumstances, which is most connected with the grosser and more animal portion of our nature' (*The Rambler*).

However, some reviewers grudgingly acknowledged a misused talent: '... considerable abilities ill applied. There is power, effect, and even nature, though of an extreme kind' (*The Spectator*). One critic, while complaining of the book's 'naked vice', admitted: 'All the characters are drawn with great power and precision of outline and the scenes are as vivid as life itself' (*North American Review*, August 1849).

*** *SUMMARY* * * *

- Charlotte's *Jane Eyre* was well received, though it shocked some people.

- Most critics were baffled or appalled by *Wuthering Heights*. Some called it 'powerful'.

- *Wildfell Hall* shocked a lot of people, received relatively few reviews, but sold well.

7 Modern Critical Approaches

A development in Brontë criticism since the 1850s has been the rise in Emily's status relative to Charlotte. Charlotte has been a particular inspiration to feminist critics. A more recent development has been an increased appreciation of Anne Brontë.

EMILY BRONTË

The 1930s saw the emergence of **new criticism**. Psychological and sociological contexts were played down in favour of an appreciation of the work's construction. There was also a new interest in the moral values of literature. In England, these approaches came together in the *Scrutiny* circle. *Wuthering Heights* was praised for its structure and its paradoxes, but the circle's principal spokesman, F.R. Leavis, could

not accept it as part of the 'Great Tradition' of English novels, calling it 'a kind of sport'.

Liberal humanism

Liberal humanist criticism assumes that there is broad agreement on what is human and on moral and aesthetic values. It concentrates on 'human truth' rather than on technical issues. One exponent of this approach is Q.D. Leavis, wife of F.R. Leavis. She is convinced that Emily Brontë intended to convey a moral message. However, she takes issue with the tendency to interpret every feature of Emily's novel as a sign of its genius.

Q.D. Leavis claims that some of the complexity in *Wuthering Heights* is really just a muddle resulting from Emily's inexperience. By this way of thinking, Emily began with a version of the *King Lear* sub-plot, coupled with an exploration of the Romantic theme of incest (in Heathcliff and Catherine), then changed tack, leaving herself with inconsistencies: Catherine relates to Heathcliff as a brother; to him they are lovers. To Leavis, Heathcliff is enigmatic only because of his creator's indecision. In spite of this criticism, Leavis praises the character of Nelly as a portrayal of motherly womanhood.

Leavis places the novel in a sociological and historical context, anticipating **new historicism**. She holds that Emily, influenced by the novels of Walter Scott, takes the theme of the corruption of childhood by society, and relates it to the gradual supplanting of the 'old rough farming culture based in a naturally patriarchal family life', with its wholesome values, by a new and 'unnatural', unhealthy class-consciousness. This in Leavis's view makes *Wuthering Heights* a responsible novel.

Pluralism

Keith Sagar, in *The Originality of Wuthering Heights*, presents one popular version of **pluralism** when he argues that Heathcliff functions on three levels simultaneously: as living proof of the evil effects of cruelty and neglect on children; as a critic of the 'unnatural' refinement of the Lintons; and as a man destroyed by his own hatred.

Frank Kermode's pluralism is much influenced by **structuralism**. Hence he looks at *Wuthering Heights* in terms of its opposites – light and dark, life and death, nature and culture. Kermode questions Q.D. Leavis's humanist assumptions, saying instead that the extreme

KEYWORDS

New historicism: movement in the 1980s which held that literary texts had to be seen in relation to the power relations of their historical context, and that there can be no historical certainty. It was a reaction against purely linguistic forms of criticism.

Pluralism: critical standpoint according to which a literary text can have many equally valid meanings.

Structuralism: Movement originating in the works of Lévi-Strauss and Barthes. It combines anthropology and linguistics. It holds that cultural behaviours have a 'grammar' similar to that of language, and that their meanings are socially constructed. Words and symbols are only meaningful in terms of their opposites.

and irreconcilable opposites in the novel create a need to find 'solutions', but that each reader supplies different solutions. What Leavis saw as false starts, Kermode sees as raising the novel to the status of a 'classic', which he defines as one which will always signify more than is needed by any one reader or generation of readers.

Kermode focuses on the importance of names and identities in the novel, taking as an example the names that Lockwood finds written in the margins of a book at the Heights: Catherine Earnshaw, Catherine Heathcliff, Catherine Linton. Read from left to right they tell the life story of the first Catherine, in the reverse order that of her daughter. This also reflects on Catherine's enquiries into her own identity. Kermode identifies Lockwood's attempts at decipherment of these names, and of the family relations at the Heights, with our own as readers.

Kermode says that Emily has deliberately left her readers to deal with the 'indeterminacies' in the plot in their own way. By way of explanation, he cites Lockwood's two dreams – of Branderham and of Catherine, which he sees as open-ended parts of the narrative rather than as clear-cut keys to understanding it. Even the ending, with the little boy reporting that he has seen the ghosts of Heathcliff and Catherine, is open to interpretation – including the possibility that Nelly's account is unreliable.

Framing and deconstruction

One step on from the idea that the text is a 'nut' to be cracked, with a single truth to extract (Leavis), or a cornucopia of valid truths (Kermode), is the **deconstructionist** approach, which says there is no ultimate truth in the text at all: the truth is determined by our choice, although there may be a degree of consensus among readers from one culture.

> **KEYWORD**
>
> Deconstruction: A critical approach invented by Jacques Derrida. It states that although structuralism claims to analyse texts in terms of their binary opposites, in practice, our hidden value-judgements always favour one element (e.g. 'light' rather than 'dark'), and that therefore meaning is a matter of choice.

The deconstructionist critic John Matthews identifies the importance of boundaries in *Wuthering Heights*, referring to Dorothy van Ghent's work on the symbolism of windows and doors in this novel, among other things representing 'interior' and 'exterior'. Matthews relates this to the narrative structure which 'frames' the story, by which Lockwood tells us what Nelly tells him. Matthews points out that there is no reason to regard either as reliable, or as separate from the story told. Both are selective and present their own versions of events. In their telling they reveal qualities and emotions that are integral to the core story – such as the desire for revenge, as when Lockwood is pleased when young Cathy is hit by Hareton.

Matthews is unconvinced by Catherine's argument that she cannot marry Heathcliff because it would degrade her. He claims that the lovers maintain the barriers between them, for the reason that there is no acceptable form for their bond to take. Marriage would not be adequate, and they cannot regain childhood paradise – if indeed it ever existed. In connection with this, he joins several other critics in identifying a theme of incest taboo. It is as if in this novel the yearning of separation is more desirable than fulfilment.

Matthews also criticizes the idea that Heathcliff represents simply the attack of nature on culture, pointing out (as does Jacobs, below) that Heathcliff becomes, on one level, quite refined, and keeps to the letter of the law in all his conniving dealings – except when he abducts young Cathy. His violence is that inherent in the social order.

Naomi Jacobs is another critic who investigates framing in this novel, but she relates it to gender, as have a number of feminist critics. She argues that in both *Wuthering Heights* and *Wildfell Hall* the enclosing narrative structure serves several functions: it represents a process undergone by both author and reader, of passing through the official reality in order to get at the truth which culture denies; it shows how domestic reality is obscured by conventional perception; and it stands for the cultural split between the sexes which is partly to blame for the tragedy of the story.

Liberal humanists: there is a key to the novel. Pluralists: there are many keys. Deconstructionists: there is no key.

Marxist views

The best-known **Marxist criticism** of *Wuthering Heights* is a critique by Terry Eagleton, who says that *Wuthering Heights* confronts the irreconcilability of passion and society. He sees Catherine's choice of Edgar over Heathcliff as pivotal to the plot of the novel. In Eagleton's view, this is a betrayal – as Heathcliff claims it is. Like Lucy Snowe in *Villette*, Catherine tries to lead two lives: a devotion of her very being to Heathcliff, and a marriage to Edgar.

KEYWORD

Marxist criticism: based on the political theories of Karl Marx and Friedrich Engels. A Marxist approach to literature insists that ideology (particularly social class) has a major influence on both what is written and what is read.

Coming to the Heights from the unknown, outside world, Heathcliff represents both an opportunity and a threat. To Catherine he is the former, but to Hindley he is clearly the latter. In the world of Charlotte Brontë, the severing of family ties enables you to climb the social ladder, but in *Wuthering Heights*, when Catherine loses her father she begins to be dragged down by Heathcliff, sharing in his degradation. When the two children visit Thrushcross Grange and peer though the window at its chandeliers and spoiled, bickering children, we see the normally concealed violence of the Establishment unleashed in the form of Skulker the bulldog. The violence of the Establishment seizes Catherine and she loses much of her wild, natural power.

Eagleton calls the relationship between Heathcliff and Catherine 'pre-social' or 'non-social'; it represents the only way they can be authentically themselves in an exploitative world. Whereas in Charlotte Brontë's novels love leads couples into society (though this is disputable – witness Jane and Rochester hidden away in Ferndean), in *Wuthering Heights* it forces them into a mythological world. They seek to preserve what Eagleton sees as the 'pre-social harmony' preceding 'the fall into history and oppression', but they can only do this mythically. Eagleton says that in presenting this view, Emily goes beyond the usual Romantic view of the noble individual resisting oppression, into a universality whose price is social exclusion.

In one sense, says Eagleton, the novel contrasts nature and society; in another it sees society as 'naturally' savage. Heathcliff is split because there is no possibility of compromise. His rise to power represents both the rise of the oppressed against the capitalist oppressor, and the victory of capitalist property-dealing over the traditional yeoman economy (as mentioned by Leavis; see above).

Psychoanalytical approaches

Some critics have applied psychological theories (**psychoanalytical criticism**), including those of Freud, Jung and Winnicott, to *Wuthering Heights*. These can be applied to individual characters, to characters and other elements in the novel as if they were deliberate symbols, or to the novel as an expression of Emily Brontë's unconscious.

One such critic, Stevie Davies, focuses on the 'language of familial desire' in the novel. She claims that Emily Brontë refused to make the compromise involved in 'growing up' into the adult world of society, and that her characters and their language reflect this. Thus, *Wuthering Heights* embodies, if not a single fall from the pre-conscious, pre-social paradise of unity (which Emily often seeks in her poems), then a series of falls in which its characters lose their joy and vivacity step by step: birth, weaning, loss of the mother, then the father, sibling rivalry, puberty, marriage, giving birth and death. All these take place in *Wuthering Heights*. She points to the infantilism of the dialogue, which is full of childish abuse, threats, demands and pleas. The massive will of the child's ego is paramount.

Davies especially comments on the language of longing, as when Catherine declares desperately to Heathcliff on her deathbed, 'I wish I could hold you … till we were both dead!' Catherine's speech, says Davies, shows a childlike terror of abandonment ('being laid alone'), rather than of death itself, and a retreat into childlike fantasy: 'That's not *my* Heathcliff.' Davies sees Heathcliff's teeth-gnashing and foaming at the mouth not as Gothic melodrama, but as a huge tantrum. She also comments on Nelly's song about a dead mother awakened in her grave by her orphaned child (compare this with Bessy's song in *Jane Eyre*), and on the moor as the natural mother to whom Heathcliff and Catherine will return.

Feminist approaches

Sandra Gilbert's chapter on *Wuthering Heights* in *The Madwoman in the Attic* discusses what she sees as Emily's preoccupation with Milton's version of the Fall as presented in *Paradise Lost*, and with heaven and hell. Catherine, for example, dreams that she does not belong in heaven (see p. 28). Gilbert sees the novel as presenting a rebellious reversal of the fall of woman and of Lucifer, whom Gilbert sees, using Jungian terminology, as women's 'shadow self'. Hence, the Heights is described in the novel as 'a perfect misanthropist's heaven' (Ch. 1).

Like other critics, including Eagleton (see above), Gilbert comments on the implicit power possessed by Thrushcross Grange, shown in the scene when Catherine is seized by the bulldog. But Gilbert sees this specifically as patriarchal power, which comes into play when Catherine reaches puberty. Gilbert comments on the blood (from the bite) symbolizing menstruation and, less convincingly, on the dog's long purple tongue and lips as phallic. From this point dates Catherine's confusion of identity. However, whereas Eagleton argues that Catherine make the wrong choice when she marries Edgar, Gilbert argues that in fact she has no choice, because she has been indoctrinated by patriarchy.

To Gilbert, whereas Catherine falls from what to her is the heaven of the Heights to the hell of Thrushcross Grange, Isabella, a child of culture, falls in the opposite direction. For Isabella, Wuthering Heights is hell, and Heathcliff is Satan. Insofar as Satan is the outcast, the underdog of heaven, he can be seen as 'female', and Gilbert sees Heathcliff in the same light. He remains illegitimate, the outsider, but in order to subvert legitimacy he impersonates it – by following the letter of the law in his dealings.

CHARLOTTE BRONTË

The influential late-Victorian critic Leslie Stephen praised Charlotte's portrayal of her narrators, but called Rochester a failure as a character: 'He is in reality the personification of a true woman's longing (may one say it now?) for a strong master.' Not surprisingly, this statement has attracted comment from feminist critics. In 1928 Virginia Woolf wrote in *A Room of One's Own* that Charlotte Brontë could never 'get her genius expressed whole and entire', because her indignation gets in the way: 'She will write in a rage where she should write calmly.' Modern criticism has come to focus more on Charlotte's representation of the female role, gender relations and power. It has largely accepted that her indignation is essential to her art.

A 'freak genius': early modern views

Some critics have said that Charlotte cannot be categorized. David Cecil praises her as the first novelist of the inner world, anticipating Joyce and Proust. Kathleen Tillotson, similarly, praises her subjective portrayal of her narrators, which she says is better than that of Dickens. However, Cecil says that her plots are full of improbabilities, and that *Jane Eyre* is 'a roaring melodrama'. Her novels, he says, are held together only by the thread of the narrator. *Villette*, he says, has for the most part a single mundane setting, yet still contrives to be improbable.

Cecil also holds that Charlotte cannot handle humour, let alone satire, pointing to the 'preposterous' dialogue given to Blanche Ingram. He even criticizes her characterization, especially that of men, and argues that in *Shirley* even the heroines are unrealistic as soon as they are alone together as friends. Against this, Cecil praises Charlotte's creative imagination: even if a scene is unrealistic, it comes alive in her hands.

M.H. Scargill excuses the improbabilities of Charlotte's plots by viewing the novels as poetry on a grand scale, in which symbolism is more important than realism.

Marxist approaches

Charlotte's novels lend themselves to Marxist interpretation as they are so obviously about power relations, and especially dominance and subservience, and have more socially inclusive settings than *Wuthering Heights*, which is to some extent in a world of its own.

Terry Eagleton takes the broad view that whereas *Wuthering Heights* refuses compromise, Charlotte's novels attempt to smooth over conflicts, achieving an uneasy compromise between social conformity and individual fulfilment. Eagleton cites the attitude of Helen Burns, in *Jane Eyre*, towards the beheading of Charles I, as reflecting the ambiguity of the novels, and Charlotte's ambivalence towards rebellion and submission. To give vent to passion too soon, he says, risks vulnerability and reprisal, as when Jane rebels and is put in the red-room. Eagleton identifies Charlotte's coping mechanism as one which delays passionate self-fulfilment, meanwhile converting submission to convention into self-advancement. Crimsworth in *The Professor* is a prime example, but Jane Eyre and Lucy Snowe behave in similar ways.

Eagleton argues that part of the process in Charlotte's novels is the marriage of bourgeois values with aristocratic ones, reflecting 'the spirit of the age'. He points to the fact that the Brontës grew up in a world in which there was a steady increase in the wealthy manufacturing middle class (which created a market for governesses). Bourgeois characters such as Hunsden in *The Professor* and Yorke in *Shirley* are 'natural aristocrats', for example in their appreciation of the arts. Crimsworth in *The Professor* sympathizes with the Whig reformer Hunsden, but does not want to destroy his own privileged world. Eagleton makes a case for *Shirley* representing the reconciliation of the old aristocracy and the new manufacturing class, as embodied in the aristocratic Shirley herself being a mill-owner and defending her manufacturing tenant Gerard Moore. Like Hunsden, Yorke is admired, but cannot be taken as a model for social change, because he lacks the veneration for the established order voiced by Mrs Pryor and felt by Charlotte herself.

Eagleton links class with gender, arguing that Charlotte's novels dramatize a society in which all relationships are power struggles. He sees Charlotte's compromising attitude towards class and social power as reflected in the sexual relationships she describes, in which there is an interplay of dominance and submission. At the end of *Jane Eyre*, for example, Jane and Rochester are equals, but he is debilitated and must depend on her, while she has chosen to become his servant. Shirley Keeldar dominates Caroline, in what Eagleton sees as a quasi-sexual relationship, but she wants to be dominated herself.

Feminist approaches

One of the most lucid feminist commentators is the poet–critic Adrienne Rich, who sees *Jane Eyre* as the life story of a woman who is incapable of saying 'I *am* Heathcliff!' (or 'I *am* Rochester!') because she is so much herself. Rich maps out the plot of *Jane Eyre* as a series of temptations, one in each new setting. In each place, Jane finds a helper who gives her strength to resist temptation to become somehow less than herself. At Thornfield, Jane resists not only moral temptation, but the urge to bond with Rochester before their relationship has matured into one in which equality is possible. Ironically, the helpers here are Bertha and Richard Mason. At Marsh End it is the Great Mother who communicates Rochester's anguish to her so that she resists the temptation to marry Rivers. Finally, her happy marriage is believable, because she has refused to accept mere myth, romance or sexual oppression.

A number of feminist approaches to Charlotte Brontë draw on psychoanalytical theory, focusing on her portrayal of the repression of female sexuality in a male-dominated world. One such approach is that of Elaine Showalter, in *A Literature of Their Own* (1978). Showalter identifies Charlotte's greatest innovation in *Jane Eyre* as the division of the female psyche into its two extreme elements of mind and body, projected in the characters of Helen Burns and Bertha Mason. Showalter explores the initiatory nature of the plot, seeing the blood drawn from Jane by John Reed as symbolizing menstruation, and her incarceration in the red-room as echoing tribal puberty rites. Showalter sees Helen as representing the female spirit in its most passive, disembodied form, and Bertha in its most terrifyingly bestial and vampirish. Showalter points out that Bertha's madness, most intense when the moon is 'blood-red and half-overcast', suggests Victorian associations between female sexuality, menstruation and madness. Both Bertha and Helen, argues Showalter, are 'killed off' when they are no longer necessary as split-off aspects of Jane's psyche, when she becomes whole.

The approach taken by Gilbert and Gubar in *The Madwoman in the Attic* (1979) has much in common with that of Showalter. It also sees Bertha as a split-off aspect of Jane, though with more emphasis on Bertha embodying Jane's rage at patriarchy, rather than her sexuality. The red-room they call a 'patriarchal death chamber', while Brocklehurst's description they judge to be phallic (he is a 'black pillar'; see Ch. 4) but also fairytale, resembling that of the wolf in Little Red Riding Hood. Their approach to *Villette* focuses on Lucy Snowe's emotional hunger, her repression of her feelings, and on the other female characters in the novel representing aspects of herself as well as role models from which she learns – even the hideous Madame Walravens. Here, again, they stress the fairytale elements of the novel. Madame Beck's house represents Lucy herself, with the attic as her unconscious.

Post-colonialist criticism

Some critics have looked at the relationship between oppression of women and glimpses of colonial oppression in Charlotte Brontë's novels, especially in *Jane Eyre* (**post-colonialism**) There are many mentions of slavery and

KEYWORD

Post-colonialism: critical movement exploring the presence (often implicit rather than explicit) of colonial elements, such as imperialism and slavery, in nineteenth-century literature. Its most well-known representative is Edward Said, who in *Orientalism* (Pantheon, 1978) argued that European literature had created a false construct of 'the oriental'.

rebellion in this novel, and Rochester's fortune comes from the West Indies' plantations, along with his wife Bertha. At the end of *Villette*, Paul Emmanuel goes to deal with business in the West Indies, suggesting that he, too, benefits from colonialism.

Gayatri Chakravorty Spivak, in *Jane Eyre: A Critique of Imperialism* (1985), discusses the marginalization of Jane in the opening scene and her rebellious behaviour. Spivak claims that in the Creole Bertha, Charlotte blurs the boundaries between human and animal enough for us to accept Bertha being supplanted, imperialistically, by Jane. Another example of imperialism is when Rivers goes to India as a missionary to 'save the natives', whether they want to be saved or not.

Susan Meyer, in Regan (ed.), *The Nineteenth-Century Novel* (2001), points to the fact that the 'Angria' of Charlotte's juvenilia was placed in Africa and shows a surprising knowledge of African history and geography, and of Caribbean slavery, including tortures used by slave-owners. Meyer places Charlotte's use of Bertha to represent 'otherness' in its context, that of British colonialism. She points to the many mentions of slavery in the novel, and of Jane's rebellion (compared in Ch. 1 to a slave revolt). Meyer holds that Charlotte begins the novel with 'an implicit critique of British domination and an identification with oppressed' but then uses slavery merely as a metaphor representing the oppression of women.

ANNE BRONTË

There has been relatively little modern criticism of Anne Brontë, though there has been some move towards a reappraisal of her work, and especially of *Wildfell Hall*. Gilbert and Gubar take issue with the view of Anne Brontë as conservatively Christian. They focus on Helen Graham's work as an artist, and how it represents the role of the female artist in a wider sense. Helen's art both expresses and conceals her identity and desires, as shown early on, when Huntingdon finds a pencil sketch of himself on the back of one of her paintings. Her paintings are 'public masks to hide her private dreams'. Her professional art is likewise both a public performance and an expression of a secret self. She signs her paintings with a false name, more evidence of her need for concealment, which reflects Charlotte's own views of a woman's need to conceal her true self for fear of patriarchal anger and reprisal.

Some feminist critics, such as Elizabeth Signoretti, observing that Helen's narrative is framed by Gilbert's, that he apparently reveals his wife's deepest secrets to his friend Halford merely to trade confidences with him, and that he reads her letters to her brother, have sensed a male conspiracy. Against this there is the view of Naomi Jacobs (see above under *Wuthering Heights*), which proposes that the framing reflects the gender division in society, as well as the process that Anne Brontë felt she had to go through in order to present her views to her reading public.

The novel also lends itself to a Marxist critique on the lines of Eagleton's critique of *Shirley* (see above). Gilbert Markham, the representative of old conservative yeoman stock, marries into the gentry, giving it a new vigour lacking in the degenerate Huntingdon. This could be seen as a plea for a freeing-up of rigid class barriers.

✳ ✳ ✳ SUMMARY ✳ ✳ ✳

- *Wuthering Heights* has received most attention. Critics have discussed its narrative framing and the mythical dimension of its characters.

- Liberal humanists have said it has a core message; pluralists have said it has many equally valid meanings; deconstructionists have said its meaning is a matter of choice.

- Critics have called Charlotte's plots improbable but admired her passion and imagination.

- Marxists see Charlotte as a compromiser, feminists as a pioneer of female emancipation.

- Post-colonial criticism has looked at the role of Bertha as an oppressed black woman.

- *Wildfell Hall* is now being reappraised. Some critics see its framing as pointing to male oppression.

8 Where Next?

READING ON

The novels

If you have read only one or two Brontë novels it is definitely worth reading more! Each of the novels also repays further reading: you will notice imagery and subtleties of language that escaped you first time round. There is no need to start at the beginning. You might want, instead, to pick out some of the outstanding passages such as those discussed at the beginning of this book. If you only ever read one chapter of *Villette* (which is, of course, worth reading in full), you might like to make it Chapter 4, focusing on Miss Marchmont, since this contains some wonderfully poetic prose, and stands well on its own. *Shirley*, though not Charlotte's best book, is entertaining, especially if you research the history. And if you have never read any Anne Brontë, read *The Tenant of Wildfell Hall*. You could also read Jean Rhys's novel *The Wide Sargasso Sea* (1966), which tells Bertha Mason's story from her point of view.

Criticism and biography

One of the most readable and insightful studies of the Brontës is found in Gilbert and Gubar, *The Madwoman in the Attic*. It contains chapters focusing on the major Brontë novels, as well putting them in context as part of the tradition of women's fiction.

The New Casebook series present a range of critical perspectives, one book dealing with *Wuthering Heights*, another with *Jane Eyre* and *Villette*. Barbara Timm Gates (ed.) *Critical Essays on Charlotte Brontë* is also good.

Reading biography is especially worthwhile in the case of the Brontës, since they are such an unusual phenomenon as a family who inspired and influenced each other. Mrs Gaskell's biography of Charlotte is very readable. You could follow up with Lucasta Miller, *The Brontë Myth*, which focuses on perceptions of the Brontës, starting with Mrs Gaskell's work. Kathryn White's *The Brontës* is a lively short biography, but Juliet Barker's is the definitive one. Edward Chitham's books on the Brontës are also very good.

HAWORTH PARSONAGE

If possible, make the 'pilgrimage' to Haworth, Yorkshire. The Parsonage is now an excellent museum, with much of the Brontës' home surroundings preserved or restored. You will see needlework to which the sisters applied themselves when they were not composing their great works, some of the clothes they wore (including Charlotte's tiny gloves and shoes), the children's nursery, Patrick's study containing the piano played mostly by Emily, and, most affectingly, the sofa on which Emily is said to have died. There are paintings by Branwell, drawings by the sisters and examples of the tiny chronicles kept by the four children. There is a library for research (by appointment).

It is also worth a visit just to see the old village for yourself, feel the wind from the moor, muse on what thoughts the overflowing graveyard might have inspired in the sisters as they gazed out of the window, and even try a pint of the appropriately named Black Sheep bitter in the Black Bull, the local pub in which Branwell spent much of his time drinking himself to death. Across the street is the apothecary's where he bought his laudanum.

One thing at least has changed, testifying to the wide appeal of the Brontës. Many signs, including footpath signs on the moor, are now in Japanese!

The museum is open all year. Contact:
The Brontë Parsonage Museum, Haworth, Keighley W. Yorks BD22 8DR, England.
Tel. +44 (0)1535 642323   Fax. +44 (0)1535 647131
Email: bronte@bronte.org.uk   Website: www.bronte.info

THE BRONTË SOCIETY

The Parsonage Museum is run by the Brontë Society, which was founded in 1893. Benefits of membership include free entry to the museum. The society organizes seminars, talks and filmshows. Find out more on its website (see above). The site is also the best place to find links to other Brontë websites.

FILMS

There are a number of films of Brontë books available on video and DVD. Novels covered are: *Wuthering Heights*, *Jane Eyre* and *The Tenant of Wildfell Hall*. Films can be a good way into the books, but there is the danger that they will preclude you imagining the characters in your own way. It can be interesting to see what directors change. For example, one good production, starring Tara Fitzgerald, introduces into the story new but effective scenes in which the father introduces the son to blood sports, leading him to torture and kill a pet bird. This alludes to the scene in *Agnes Grey* in which Agnes kills a nest of thrushes rather than let the indulged son of the family torture them.

✳ ✳ ✳ SUMMARY ✳ ✳ ✳

- Read the novels, some critical works and a biography.
- Visit Haworth.
- Join the Brontë Society.
- See the films.

GLOSSARY

Allegory   A story whose meaning is deliberately represented in a symbol.

Bildungsroman   A 'novel of education', especially in the German tradition, following the development of a single main protagonist through his or her life. Fielding's *Tom Jones* is an example.

Bluebeard   In the folktale, Bluebeard warns his wife never to enter a forbidden room in his castle. Overcome by curiosity, she disobeys him and finds it contains the corpses of his previous wives.

Byronic hero   Typically a proud, brooding man, of superior intellect and sensitivity, often tormented by some dark sexual crime in his past, yet rebelliously refusing to repent; based, in part, on Milton's Lucifer.

Deconstruction   A critical approach invented by Jacques Derrida. It states that although structuralism claims to analyse texts in terms of their binary opposites, in practice, our hidden value-judgements always favour one element (e.g. 'light' rather than 'dark'), and that therefore meaning is a matter of choice.

Dramatic irony   When the reader (or audience) is aware of an important fact of which one character is unaware.

Fairytale   A story involving magical beings and events.

Gothic   Descriptive of a novel or poem focusing on the stranglehold of the past on the present, and containing suggestions of the supernatural. In the English Gothic tradition, these turn out to have rational explanations.

Marxist criticism   Based on the political theories of Karl Marx and Friedrich Engels. A Marxist approach to literature insists that ideology (particularly social class) has a major influence on both what is written and what is read.

Metaphor   An image (word picture) in which something is spoken of as if it were something essentially different but in some way similar.

Mother goddess   In pagan religion, a goddess representing nature as a mother.

Myth   An ancient story involving deities which personify aspects of the universe, the human mind, and the human situation.

New criticism   Movement which saw literary works as artefacts, to be appreciated for themselves as unities of paradox and ambiguity, not as 'messages' from the author.

New historicism   Movement in the 1980s which held that literary texts had to be seen in relation to the power relations of their historical context, and that there can be no historical certainty. It was a reaction against purely linguistic forms of criticism.

Personification   A kind of metaphor in which something is described as if it were a person.

Pluralism   Critical standpoint according to which a literary text can have many equally valid meanings.

Post-colonialism   Critical movement exploring the presence (often implicit rather than explicit) of colonial elements, such as imperialism and slavery, in nineteenth-century literature. Its most well-known representative is Edward Said, who in *Orientalism* (Pantheon, 1978) argued that European literature had created a false construct of 'the oriental'.

Psyche   The mind, including all that is repressed or projected onto others.

Psychoanalytical criticism Criticism based on the theories of Sigmund Freud and those influenced by him, identifying elements of a text as representing aspects of the author's psyche, especially repressed forces in the unconscious.

Romance   A novel or poem which is fantastical and focuses on high emotions rather than everyday reality.

Romantics   The followers of a movement in the arts which reacted to the rationalist Age of Enlightenment and the Industrial Revolution. The movement emphasized the freedom of the individual, the power of nature, equality and the irrational.

Structuralism Movement originating in the work of Lévi-Strauss and Barthes. It combines anthropology and linguistics. It holds that cultural behaviours have a 'grammar' similar to that of language, and that their meanings are socially constructed. Words and symbols are only meaningful in terms of their opposites.

Symbolism The use of one thing to represent something else.

CHRONOLOGY OF MAJOR WORKS

1846	*Poems* by 'Currer, Ellis and Acton Bell'
1847	*Jane Eyre* (October), *Wuthering Heights* and *Agnes Grey* (December)
1848	*The Tenant of Wildfell Hall*
1849	*Shirley*
1853	*Villette*
1857	*The Professor* (written before *Jane Eyre*)

FURTHER READING

Allott, M. (ed.), *Charlotte Brontë: Jane Eyre and Villette* (London: Macmillan, 1973).

Barker, J., *The Brontës* (London: Phoenix Press, 1994).

Chitham, E., *A Life of Anne Brontë* (Oxford, Blackwell, 1991).

Davies, P., *The Brontës* (London: Greenwich Exchange, 2000).

Davies, S., *The Brontë Sisters: Selected Poems* (Cheadle: Carcanet, 1999).

Eagleton, T., *Myths of Power: A Marxist Study of the Brontës* (London: Macmillan, 1988).

Gaskell, E., *The Life of Charlotte Brontë* (Oxford: Oxford University Press, 1996).

Gilbert, S. and Gubar, S., *The Madwoman in the Attic* (New Haven, CT, and London: Yale University Press, 1979).

Lemon, C. (ed.), *Classics of Brontë Scholarship* (Keighley: Brontë Society, 1999).

Lloyd Evans, B., and Lloyd Evans, G., *Everyman's Companion to the Brontës* (London: Dent, 1982).

Miller, L., *The Brontë Myth* (London: Vintage, 2002).

O'Neill, J., *The World of the Brontës* (London: Carlton, 1997).

Regan, S. (ed.), *The Nineteenth-Century Novel: A Critical Reader* (London: Routledge, 2001).

Rich, A., *On Lies, Secrets, and Silence, Selected Prose 1966–1978* (New York: Norton, 1979).

Showalter, E., *A Literature of Their Own* (London: Virago, 1978).

Stoneman, P. (ed.), *Wuthering Heights* (London: Macmillan, 1993).

Timm Gates, B., *Critical Essays on Charlotte Brontë* (Boston, MA: G.K. Hall, 1990).

White, K., *The Brontës* (Stroud: Sutton, 1998).

Woolf, V., *A Room of One's Own* (Harmondsworth: Penguin, 1945).

INDEX